PRAISE FOR WOMEN'S INTEREST

"We, as women, are being given a treasure trove of information in [this book].... It stands to bring humor and shed light on millions."

—**Erin Barrett, author of *Random Kinds of Factness***

"Alicia Alvarez's deep research and work in women's studies has been a major influence on the world. What sets her books apart is that they are as enlightening as they are entertaining."

—**Becca Anderson, author of *The Book of Awesome Women***

"An engaging and entertaining workout for the mind! Get ready to learn the quirkiest of facts and trivia with this book."

—**Sophie Stirling, author of *We Did That?***

"What a fun collection of interesting facts and trivia. I learned something new each time I opened this book!"

—**Marina Greenway, author of *Listify***

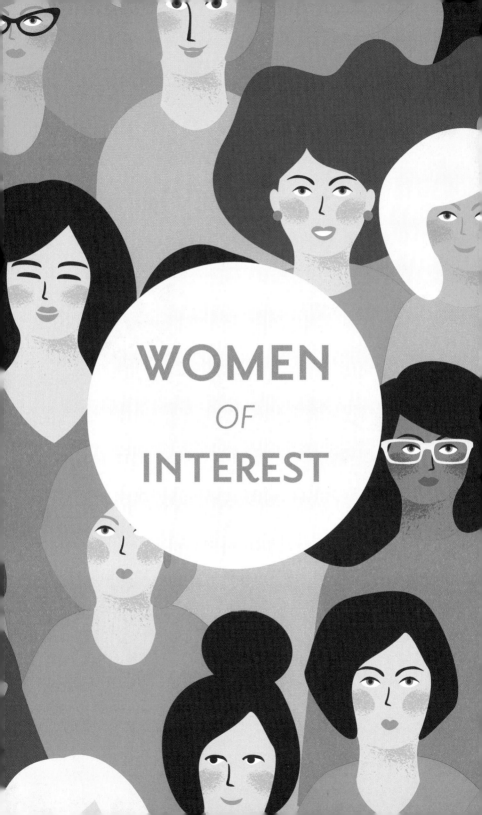

WOMEN

OF

INTEREST

WOMEN

OF

INTEREST

The Ultimate Book
of Women's Trivia

ALICIA ALVREZ

Foreword by Erin Barrett,
author of *Random Kinds of Factness*

Conari
Press

CORAL GABLES

This edition was first published in 2008 by Red Wheel/Weiser, LLC, under the imprint of Conari Press, as *The Big Book of Women's Trivia*

Published by Mango Publishing Group, a division of Mango Media Inc.

Cover Illustration: © Nadia Grapes/shutterstock.com
Cover Design, Layout & Design: Morgane Leoni
Interior Illustrations based on: © Nadia Grapes/shutterstock.com

For permission requests, please contact the publisher at:
Mango Publishing Group
2850 S Douglas Road, 2nd Floor
Coral Gables, FL 33134 USA
info@mango.bz

For special orders, quantity sales, course adoptions and corporate sales, please email the publisher at sales@mango.bz. For trade and wholesale sales, please contact Ingram Publisher Services at customer.service@ingramcontent.com or +1.800.509.4887.

Women of Interest: The Ultimate Book of Women's Trivia

Library of Congress Cataloging-in-Publication number: 2020946296
ISBN: (print) 978-1-64250-366-1, (ebook) 978-1-64250-367-8
BISAC category code REF023000—REFERENCE / Trivia

Printed in the United States of America

This book is dedicated to the women who came before us and paved the way.

Women rule!

Contents

FOREWORD

W ell, ladies, our day is finally here. "In a trivia book?" you may ask. Let me explain.

For centuries, women have been the storytellers, the information seekers and keepers, the wellspring of knowledge, dispensing it as the archetypal wisewomen. But all too often in our modern-day culture, women get passed by for men in the realm of trivia.

What do I mean? Take Cliff Clavin from the TV hit *Cheers*, the quintessential trivia buff. Can you think of an iconic female pop-culture equivalent? No. Over and over, men are depicted as the holders of minutiae, while we women quietly sit on the sidelines soaking in knowledge, unobserved, overlooked, but growing secretly smarter and smarter.

Thanks to Alicia Alvrez, however, that pop-culture paradigm is being turned on its head. Not only are we as women being given a treasure trove of information in *Women of Interest*, but it's the kind of information about our *lives*: who we are, what we love, what makes us tick.

For instance, women invented all of the following: the bulletproof vest, the fire escape, windshield wipers, and the laser printer. And who'd have guessed that female nurses earn about 5 percent *more* than their male counterparts? Or that osculation could be so fun and burn so many calories? (Keep reading!)

But it's not just that. Ms. Alvrez, understanding that over 55 percent of all US purchases are controlled by women, has made a shrewd move by devoting this book to knowledge-seeking women everywhere. It stands to bring humor and shed light on millions. Clearly, she's a source to be trusted, dear readers, a guidepost on our information journey.

So, as you read this book, take these information morsels, taste them. Roll them around on your tongue. Digest them. Remember: information becomes knowledge. Knowledge becomes wisdom. Wisdom is powerful. Powerful is woman. The *sistahs* are doin' it for themselves!

Read on,

ERIN BARRETT
Author of *Random Kinds of Factness*

CHAPTER 1

Women and Their Wardrobes

We've always loved to accessorize. Archeologists have uncovered bracelets made of mammoth bones from 20,000 BC and necklaces of mammoth tusks, shells, and animal teeth from 30,000 BC.

Is shopping in the female genes? No one knows for sure, but what is known is that deprived of the money to shop, women will keep on shopping anyway. Women outnumber men by five to one in shoplifting convictions.

And speaking of trends, the craze for shaved armpits in women began in the United States around 1920, when deodorant began being marketed and bathing suits that revealed one's armpits became fashionable.

Bottoms Up

As you know, pants were originally a male-only fashion item. But so were undies. Women, no matter the circumstances, were just supposed to keep their skirts down and avoid showing their bottoms to the world. Indeed, it was a crime to let anyone other than your husband see your privates. This caused quite a problem for Catherine de' Medici, who loved to ride horseback. Every time her horse jumped, she broke the law. What was a gal to do? She was damned either way—either she could continue to be immodest or don some coverings. But that caused consternation too, with one critic proclaiming, "Women should leave their buttocks uncovered under their skirts, they should not appropriate a masculine garment but leave their behinds nude as is suitable for them." It wasn't until the mid-1800s that women began wearing underpants on a regular basis.

By the way, Catherine took up riding because it was a way of showing off her legs, which were her best feature. It is she who is credited with having invented riding sidesaddle for women, again for the advantage of showing off her legs.

A Fashion Trend I'm Glad I Missed

It used to be fashionable in the late 1800s and early 1900s for women to shave off their eyebrows and wear glued-on mouse fur ones instead.

Before the 1920s, tanned skin was considered coarse because it was associated with working class people who got tanned by working outside. That all changed when the famous designer Coco Chanel returned from a cruise on the Duke of Westminster's private yacht with a tan. Suddenly, everyone had to have one, and sales of parasols and bonnets dried up.

Speaking of parasols and the like, umbrellas first made an appearance in China in the second century BC.

Emily Post on Proper Fashion, Circa 1922

- "What makes a brilliant party? Clothes. Good clothes. A frumpy party is nothing more nor less than a collection of badly dressed persons."

- "Rather be frumpy than vulgar! ... Frumps are often celebrities in disguise—but a person of vulgar appearance is vulgar all through."

- It's important to be chic, said she; "Chic is a borrowed adjective, but there is no English word to take the place of elegant, which was destroyed utterly by the reporter or practical joker who said, 'elegant dresses.' "

"Fashion ought to be likened to a tide or epidemic; sometimes one might define it as a sort of hypnotism, seemingly exerted by the gods as a joke."

"All women who have any clothes sense whatsoever know more or less the type of things that are their style— unless they have such an attack of fashionitis as to be irresponsibly delirious."

"A conspicuous evidence of bad style that has persisted through numberless changes in fashion is the over-dressed and over-trimmed head."

Those who received her greatest disdain were modern women with overly fancy shoes and fur coats. "She much prefers wearing rings to gloves. Maybe she thinks they do not go together? ... She also cares little (apparently) for staying at home, since she is perpetually seen at restaurants and at every public entertainment. The food she orders is rich, the appearance she makes is rich; in fact, to see her often is like nothing so much as being forced to eat a large amount of butter—plain."

"When in doubt, wear the plainer dress. It is always better to be under-dressed than over-dressed."

In the 1930s, members of the British Royal Air Force were introduced to a new kind of inflatable life jacket. They named it the "Mae West," for the remarkably busty actress who was then at the height of her popularity, because the jacket gave the wearer a busty profile.

Do you own a Victorian, a.k.a. a tippy? That's a scarf of fur (or now, fake fur) that has long, dangly ends. It's named, not surprisingly, for Queen Victoria.

Emergency Fashion Tips

Hem come loose and no thread in sight? Try masking tape or
a stapler.

Bring your patent leather shoes back to life with petroleum jelly.
Rub a pea-sized amount into the leather.

Use a black felt-tipped laundry marker to cover over cracks
in black leather shoes or to cover a light-colored stain on any
black cloth.

No, freezing your panty hose will not keep a run from spreading,
but clear nail polish will.

The Marquise de Pompadour was the mistress of Louis XV and
was so influential that the other ladies of the French court would
rapidly follow whatever fashion she adopted. So when she began
to appear with her hair piled astonishingly high on her head, the
multitudes followed suit; hence the name "pompadour" for that
particular hairdo.

Fingernail Facts

Your fingernails and toenails are a type of skin that grows about
one inch per year. The record for the longest fingernails on both
hands is held by a woman living in Salt Lake City, Utah, whose
nails are a whopping twenty-four inches long.

If you are less than happy about the state of your nails,
remember that the fashion of long, perfect nails developed

among wealthy ladies of leisure who had not much else to do with their time than to spend it having their nails done.

It is the fashion in many countries to grow one fingernail to show you don't have to do manual labor. Which nail it is varies— in the Philippines, it's the thumbnail; in Greece, it's the pinky.

Ancient Egyptians, ahead in this as in so many things, were among the first people to use fingernail polish—they would color their nails with henna. The ancient Chinese dyed their nails too—with vegetable dyes mixed with beeswax, among other things.

When polish was first introduced in the United States in 1907, women's magazines published directions on how to put it on.

A Fashion Faux Pas

In 1994, couturier Karl Lagerfeld created a slinky black dress with a love poem in Arabic as a design element on the front. He should have done his research better—the passage turned out to be from the Koran, which created a huge stir in the Muslim community when it appeared on the runway that season. The designer apologized, destroying not only the dress but all photos and videos of it as well.

In the early 1900s, it was fashionable to brush on your powder with a rabbit's foot.

Anthropologists tell us that all cultures around the world from 15,000 BC onward invented some kind of comb to get the tangles out of hair. All but one, that is—the Britons, who had unruly heads until AD 789, when the Danes invaded and taught them proper grooming techniques.

Archeologists once found a solid gold comb in a tomb on the Black Sea.

In ancient Japan, the kind of ornaments you wore in your hair revealed your class, age, and marital status.

Highly prized hairpins in China had blue kingfisher bird feathers in them. They were so valued that they were sent to the emperor as tribute. Chinese women would also wear hairpins with springs that bobbed every time they moved their heads.

Mattel has done studies of what girls actually do with Barbies. Far and away, the most common activity is playing with their hair.

European royalty began the fashion of wig wearing in the seventeenth century because two kings—Louis XIV and Charles II—didn't want anyone to see their natural hair, Louis because he had none, and Charles because his was gray. Wearing wigs became so fashionable that in the eighteenth century, children were in danger of having their hair cut off as they played outside and houses were built with racks for guests' wigs to be stored on. The trend ended with the Revolutionary War, when it became decidedly unfashionable to follow the fashions of royalty.

Hats Off to Him

Guido Orlando was a very creative marketing professional who was employed in the late 1950s by the Millinery Institute of America to get women to buy more hats. Knowing that the Catholic Church required women to cover their heads at mass, Orlando wrote a letter to the pope on letterhead from a bogus organization called the Religious Research Institute, saying that a survey showed that over twenty million women in North America went to weekly mass with bare heads (a "fact" which he had made up). Then Orlando offered a remedy that the pope might want to suggest to his flock: "Of the various pieces of apparel worn by women today, hats do the most to enhance the dignity and decorum of womanhood. It is traditional for hats to be worn by women in church and on other religious occasions— and I commend hats as a right and proper part of women's dress." His scheme worked. Pope Pius used Orlando's very words in a general recommendation, and hat sales soared.

Hatter to the Stars

Mildred Blount was an African American woman who was the hatter to the stars in 1930s New York. She created an exhibition of hats based on designs from 1690 through 1900 that was shown at the 1939 New York World's Fair, and she was tapped to design the hats for the movie *Gone with the Wind*. Women like Rosalind Russell, Joan Crawford, Gloria Vanderbilt, Marian Anderson, and many wealthy black women became her clients. One of her hats was featured on the August 1942 cover of *Ladies' Home Journal*. In 1943, she became the first black American to have her work exhibited at the famous Medcalf's Restaurant in Los Angeles.

We in the United States spend over five billion dollars annually on perfumes and colognes.

When perfume techniques were more primitive, it took two hundred pounds of roses to make one ounce of rose scent.

For thousands of years, women poisoned themselves with their face makeup by using ceruse, a powder that caused lead poisoning. Rouge, too, was not safe—it contained mercury, which led to miscarriages and birth defects.

"I would never stoop so low as to be fashionable."

—Dolly Parton

In England in the late 1700s, there was a law that said women could not lure men into marriage by using makeup. To do so was to be branded a witch.

In the original story, Cinderella didn't wear glass slippers (which makes sense—glass would break). She wore squirrel fur slippers. But the person who translated the tale from French to English confused *pantouffles en vair* with *pantouffles en verre*, and glass it became.

Blue jeans are named for the fabric they are made of. The word *jean* is a derivation of Genoa, which is the city in Italy where the material came from. Denim too gets its name from its city of origin—Nimes in France. The fabric was called in French *serge de Nimes*, which English speakers mangled into *denim*.

Actually, what we call "paper" money is made of a denimlike cotton as well as linen, which makes it much more durable than regular paper.

Mood Swings

According to the Color Marketing Group, what colors are in at any given moment is a reflection of the economic times. When the economy is booming, we flock to bright colors like bright orange, gold, and red; when times get tough, we gravitate to beige, brown, and cream. One reason why, they say, is that we are less likely to buy an appliance that is chartreuse, for instance, if we think we will have to keep it for a long time. If we're confident in our ability to get a new one when we feel like it, we're more adventurous. Colorists say pink will be the color of this decade, in all kinds of shades ranging from orchid to "Millennial pink."

The fashion for hairlessness on women's bodies goes back to ancient India. Since then, hair on legs and underarms has gone in and out of fashion.

Those who track such things tell us that women break down into three categories of preferred method of leg hair removal: 50 percent like shaving; 25 percent go for waxing; and 25 percent prefer depilatory creams. This of course excludes the 5 percent of women who opt to leave their leg hair as is.

Bizarre Bras

Emily Duffy, a female sculpture artist in San Francisco, California, created an 1,800-pound Bra Ball constructed out of over seven thousand donated bras.

In 1979, a bra called the Loving Cup was introduced. It could be programmed around one's menstrual cycle so that it would flash a red or green light as to whether the wearer was in her fertile period or not.

Edible bras made a brief appearance in the '70s. Flavors included cherry and licorice.

We used to use Band-Aids to cover our nipples while going braless, but the French in the 1980s did one better. They created the Joli'bust, which were two strips of adhesive to be placed under the breasts to create uplift.

Someone once created a diamond bra made of 3,250 diamonds, presumably to be worn as outerwear. It cost $1.5 million.

"I have no weakness for shoes. I wear very simple shoes which are pump shoes. It is not one of my weaknesses."

—Imelda Marcos, who was found to have 3,400 pairs of shoes in her closet

Bras of the future: scented ones that will release fragrance all day; bras that will release insect repellent; and one made of hologrammatic material that will project better looking breasts than you have. I'm waiting for the Smart Bra, made of shape-changing materials that will fit you exactly!

More Bra News

At a professional golf tournament in the '70s, a player hit a ball into a woman's bra. She was allowed to remove it, and the golfer continued on with play.

In ancient Assyria, locks were considered fashionable only if curled. So both women and men would use iron bars that had been heated to curl their hair.

The earliest hair dryer was marketed as part of a vacuum cleaner—women were pictured drying their hair in the hot air the vacuum gave off.

The Mother of Invention

Bermuda shorts were invented as a solution to a morals issue. In the 1940s, a law was passed on the island of Bermuda saying that women were not allowed to walk around with bare legs. So knee-length shorts, which were worn with knee socks, were born.

Emilio Pucci was a fashion designer in the '50s who was on the Isle of Capri when he spied a woman in skintight calf-length pants. And Capri pants were born.

The bob haircuts of the Roaring Twenties gave their name to the hair clips used to hold them back—bobby pins.

The bestselling mascara in the world is Maybelline's Great Lash. One is bought somewhere in the world every 1.9 seconds.

Over 50 percent of the women in the United States use hair coloring. Men are dyeing, too, but over half of them say they were talked into it by the women in their lives.

Some early hair dyes: crushed dried tadpoles in oil in ancient Egypt; black wine, raw crow's egg, and putrefied leeches in ancient Rome.

Bad news on the lipstick front (although you might have guessed as much): Only 50 percent of our lipstick stays on our lips; the rest we end up accidentally eating.

More Fashion Advice from Emily Post

Since in Ms. Post's estimation, freckles were the very worst thing that can happen to a woman (she called them "as violent as they are hideous"), she counseled wearing an orange-red veil when out in the sun. Some of her commandments were more reasonable than others, like the first one here...the others, not so much:

- "One should always wear a simpler dress in one's own house than one wears in going to the house of another."

- "You must never wear an evening dress and a hat [at the same time]!"

- Because of the vulgarity of most exercise outfits, "the young woman who wants to look pretty should confine her exercise to dancing. She can also hold a parasol over her head and sit in a canoe."

- "Elderly women should not wear grass green," or "royal blue, or purple.... Pink and orchid are often very becoming to older women."

Ever notice how many zippers have YKK on them? It stands for the Japanese-owned corporation Yoshida Kogyou Kabushikkaisha, makers of 90 percent of the world's zippers.

The zipper was first created in 1917 (its creator, Gideon Sundback, nicknamed it the "snake trap") but didn't come into popularity until the 1930s. It was originally designed for men's pants, but its usefulness soon spread to all types of clothing. Of course, when it was first introduced, no one was quite sure what to do with it, so it came with instructions.

Women of the Toda tribe in southern India have only two items of clothing their whole life. One they get as children; the other as young women.

In the nineteenth century, it was fashionable for ladies of certain means to have makeup tattooed on their lips and cheeks. In the twenty-first century, that practice has been revived. Recently I met someone who had had lipstick and eyeliner tattooed on. Yes, she revealed, it hurt like hell to do.

Four percent of women in the United States own no undergarments (by choice, I gather), and 6 percent sleep nude.

Have you ever heard the expression "pin money" to describe a housewife's allowance? I thought it always referred to the smallness of the amount—that you could only purchase a pin with it. But no. It turns out that pins were first created in the 1500s and were very rare and expensive because they were made of silver. In England, there was even a monopoly controlling the price and quantity, and pins were available for purchase only two days in January. When January rolled around, husbands would give their wives pin money to purchase these luxury items.

Muumuus are probably the only fashion item ever to be designed by Christian missionaries. Distraught over the Hawaiians' tendency to run around butt naked, they quickly did up some shapeless gowns to cover the women. In fact, the word means "cut off" in Hawaiian, referring to the way it seems cut off at the neck.

Sunglasses were a fifteenth-century Chinese invention. They were worn by judges to hide their reactions in court.

Diamonds didn't become a girl's best friend until the thirteenth century. Before that, they were for men only. That changed when a lady friend of the king of France demanded that she be allowed a sparkly bauble, too.

Know how to tell real pearls from fake? Run your teeth very gently across them. Fake feel smooth; the real things feel a bit rough. The technique comes to us from one Arthur Barry, a famous thief in the 1920s, who claimed to have stolen more than $500,000 a year during his career. One of the most famous heists he ever pulled off was the Plaza Hotel Robbery, when he got away with $750,000 worth of jewels belonging to the daughter of the Woolworth fortune while she was in the bathtub only a few feet away from him.

Humans began wearing clothes around the year 30,000 BC, based on the evidence in bas-relief sculpture. And woven linen, wool, and cotton fabric fragments from 6000 BC have been unearthed by anthropologists.

Before 3,400 BC, shoes were made out of papyrus by the Egyptians. Then they gravitated toward sturdier material—sandals of woven reed or leather.

"They were doing a full back shot of me in a swimsuit and I thought, oh my God, I have to be so brave."

—Cindy Crawford

So We Can Shop 'Til We Drop

The first credit card in the world was Diners Club, which was first issued in 1950. The first bank card was Bank of America's in 1958.

Many married women could not get credit cards issued in their own names as late as 1967, despite many government measures to increase women's economic freedom at that time.

If Hair Could Talk

According to a recent study commissioned by Physique, a hair products line, women with:

- Long, straight blonde hair (think Jennifer Aniston) are considered the wealthiest and most sexy.

- Short, tousled hairstyles (like Meg Ryan) are thought to be outgoing and self-assured.

- Medium-length, casual cuts (Sandra Bullock, for example) are seen as being smarter and more easygoing.

No great marketing decisions went into the name of the most famous jeans in the world—Levi 501s. "501" was just their stock number. When Levi Strauss, a real-life guy from San Francisco, first made them, he didn't like the word *jeans*. He called them "waist-high overalls."

According to US government figures, 150,000 folks get injured by their clothes annually. How is not revealed—zippers probably figure prominently.

Anne Klein's real name is Hannah Goloski.

Fashion Fads

By the 1930s, fashions had loosened up a lot since Victorian times. But there was one body part that still was not exposed—the back. That changed the day Tallulah Bankhead wore a backless dress in 1932's *Thunder Below*. Suddenly they were everywhere, as were backless swimsuits.

Minh Hanh is the most celebrated fashion designer Vietnam has ever had. She is personally credited with bringing back the *ao dai* into vogue, the traditional Vietnamese outfit consisting of a long formfitting tunic over pants. In the 1980s, she managed to make a fashion statement even with the six yards of low-quality cotton the Vietnamese government allotted per year to each citizen. And she caused quite a stir with the outfit she designed for her own wedding—a multitiered wedding dress constructed completely out of mosquito netting.

Mini Mama

Britain's Mary Quant is often credited with creating the miniskirt, though fashion pundits argue that French designer André Courrèges actually thought of it first. She certainly was the popularizer of the sensation, as the famously hip in the '60s flocked to her boutique. There is no argument, however, that she invented hot pants, and her tiny skirts led directly to the maxi-coat (to warm the legs bared by tiny skirts) and one of the most wonderful fashion innovations of all times—pantyhose.

Speaking of minis, they were considered too racy—until former first lady Jackie Kennedy was photographed wearing one to lunch. Then the fad was on!

"Elegance is the
only beauty that
never fades."

—Audrey Hepburn

According to *1,001 MORE Facts Somebody Screwed Up*, the reason miniskirts went out of fashion the first time was not due to fickle fashionmongers. Rather, the winter of 1969 was so cold worldwide that women abandoned the tiny pieces of cloth in droves for warmer wear.

In the 1890s, nipple piercing became incredibly popular among proper Victorian ladies. The fashion was to wear matching earrings and breast rings.

According to a study by Miraclesuit, women hate shopping for bathing suits so much that 62 percent of those surveyed said it is worse than childbirth and 52 percent felt they would rather clean a litter box than look for a suit.

CHAPTER 2

The Body Beautiful— and Not So

A pproximately one in every five women suffers from migraines.

Women who stand the best chance of living to celebrate their eightieth birthdays live in Japan, France, Andorra, Switzerland, Iceland, Hong Kong, Macau, Sweden, the Netherlands, or Norway.

Men can read smaller print than women can; women can hear better.

A study in *Science* based on 280 sets of twins determined that musical ability is 80 percent genetically based and only 20 percent environmental. No wonder all those children of singers follow in mom's or pop's footsteps.

I am still not sure I believe this, but supposedly there are twenty-eight million folks who snore in the United States, divided equally between men and women. Women don't snore, do they?

The Urge to Scratch

We feel itchy when something is irritating the nerve endings on the upper layer of our skin. As mammals, we have developed scratching behavior that removes the stimulus that's causing the itch.

Headlines on Heartburn

A recent survey of the National Heartburn Alliance found that 43 percent of women between the ages of eighteen and twenty-five suffer from heartburn as much as two to four times a week. That's not good, says the Alliance. Heartburn can lead to complications such as esophageal cancer and asthma. Most folks don't know that—60 percent of those surveyed just suffer in silence.

Heartburn is the worst for pregnant women because of the space taken up by the baby.

Heartburn and other tummy upsets are said to cost fifty billion dollars a year in lost wages.

According to *Epidemiology*, left-handed women run a 42 percent greater risk of developing breast cancer than do right-handers.

80 percent of suspicious mammograms are false positives. Only 1 percent lead to biopsies.

Gradually our bodies are adapting to current living conditions. Anthropologists tell us that our little toes and appendixes are getting progressively smaller because we don't need them. Our teeth are also getting smaller as we eat more processed and cooked foods that require less tearing and chewing. Our teeth are half the size of those of Neanderthals.

When You Say You're All Thumbs, You're Saying a Lot

More of your brain is used to move your thumb than is used to control your torso or stomach.

We have an accident-prone woman to thank for the invention of Band-Aids. Well, actually, it was her husband, Earle Dickson, who got tired of having to bind up his wife's burns from cooking. He happened to work for Johnson & Johnson, and the invention he concocted for his wife has gone on to sell over a hundred billion!

An organization at Penn State University called the Tremin Trust has been tracking data on women's menstrual cycles for the past sixty years. Here's what they have to say about what's normal:

- If you are thirty years old, chances are you will have a twenty-nine-day cycle and your period will last five days. But if yours is different, there's nothing to worry about, they say, if it has always been that way. Tell your doctor about any changes in your regular cycle.

- If you are using more than one tampon per hour or two at a time, that's heavy bleeding that should be reported to your doctor.

- It is now believed that women are most fertile in their early thirties because they are ovulating most consistently then.

- While the average age for menopause is fifty-one, some women begin to make the shift a decade earlier. The term for the changes they experience is *perimenopausal*.

Tampons are not a modern notion. Ancient Egyptian women had the idea in the fifteenth century BC. They used papyrus. The ancient Romans had ones made of wool, while the Japanese used paper. But somehow the idea got lost in Europe, as many ideas did, until quite recently.

More Period News

The garment of choice for that time of month in Europe and the United States until WWI was diapers made of linen. Then nurses in France discovered bandages worked better, and the idea soon spread.

In Persia, women who menstruated more than four days were considered evil and were given a whipping of a hundred lashes.

In many pre-agrarian societies, women were segregated in separate tents or huts during menstruation because they were considered unclean and it was believed they would bring bad luck to the hunt.

It was a Denver doctor who had the idea for a modern tampon in 1931. He called his invention Tampax. He sold his idea to a company which took the name and went on to sell the items to druggists by having their salesmen pretend to be thirsty. When the salesman was given a glass of water, he would throw a tampon in to show its absorbency.

The name Tampax comes from the words *tampon* and *vaginal pack.*

Tampons were first introduced in the United States to controversy. They were considered bad by certain religious groups who thought they would deflower young girls. (They do not, by the way.)

The average woman uses 11,000 tampons in her reproductive lifetime.

If you came of age before the 1970s, you already know this, but before that decade, a woman would wear a special belt and hook a very bulky sanitary pad onto it. When the thinner pads with adhesive strips were developed, women everywhere rejoiced.

Women were cautioned by a 1901 medical guide entitled *Warren's Household Physician* never to try to stop their periods by putting their feet in cold water. It could be quite dangerous, the book claimed: "The most lovely and innocent girls have done this for the purpose of attending a party; and in some instances, the stoppage induced has ended in death within a few hours."

Manufacturers get more than $3 billion of our money each year through our purchase of "personal products."

New research may explain part of why girls do less well in math than boys do in high school, besides family and faculty members who have often been known to discourage girls' interest in STEM fields. A study in *Pediatrics* found that even low levels of iron deficiency (not low enough to show up as anemia) resulted in lower scores on standardized math tests, and teenage girls have the highest levels of iron deficiency due to menstruation.

Work stressing you out? London researchers found that levels of stress hormones are higher on weekday mornings than on weekends, as we anticipate the day ahead.

Some African women can carry up to seventy-five pounds on their heads for long distances. They start young carrying light objects to get the feel of it, and by the time they are grown, they can effortlessly carry up to 35 percent of their body weight on their heads. The trick is to create a straight line between the spine and pelvis and keep their heads and hips very still.

New research shows that you can cut your risk for colon cancer by getting your Recommended Daily Allowance of copper. Copper is found in oysters, liver, and nuts.

A Weighty Subject

So many women worry about their weight. Here is some data to put into your mental hopper:

- Women's brains weigh less than men's.

- We move around less than we did even fifty years ago, so we use three to four hundred fewer calories daily than we used to (and are consequently heavier).

- Your rate of respiration goes up after a big meal because you need more energy to digest the food in your stomach and breathing quickly helps provide that energy. So the more you eat, the more calories you burn digesting.

- A study by Vanderbilt University found that women on diets who eat three meals a day actually lose more weight than those who skip breakfast—five pounds more on average. Eating small meals throughout the day has been found to be most effective.

- The average American woman weighs 15 percent more than the typical *Playboy* centerfold.

- Perhaps you know that over half of the human body is water. But were you also aware that men's bodies contain a bit more than women's?

- Since it takes more than forty muscles to frown but only seventeen to smile, does that mean that frowning is a better way to burn calories?

- Your heart weighs one-third as much as your brain.

- You weigh a bit less at the Equator than at the North Pole because the Equator is farther from Earth's center and the pull of gravity is less.

- Those trying to lose weight with the help of online weight loss sites should note this: Researchers at Brown University found that if you do not receive personal advice, the average weight loss with such sites was four pounds in six months. Following the website's advice and e-mailing a therapist increased the loss to an average of nine pounds in the same amount of time.

- Women are considered obese when 30 percent of their body weight is fat; for men, it is 25 percent.

- Married obese women tend to have been obese before marriage.

- Here's some ways to burn calories (all are based on doing the activity for one hour): Shopping—160; riding a motorless scooter—306; wild dancing—366; sailing—183; snowshoeing with poles—685.

- Women burn fat more slowly than men, by a rate of about 50 calories—about one chocolate chip cookie's worth per day.

- Fully 95 percent of women, pregnant or not, have food cravings. Only 70 percent of men do.

If you are a migraine sufferer, chances are you have been told that eating chocolate can bring on a migraine. New research reveals, however, that the craving for chocolate is actually a symptom of the early stages of the migraine. Eating chocolate won't affect the headache one way or another, but if you take the craving as a sign to start your migraine medicine, that might help you catch it before it gets too bad.

Women crave pickles and other salty items when they are pregnant because they need 40 percent more blood to feed the placenta, and salt is a key ingredient in creating and sustaining this amount of blood. Additionally, the water the baby is floating in is actually a saline solution, and salt is needed for that, too.

"If I can't have too many truffles, I'll do without truffles."

—Colette, the famous French novelist

Why, oh why, if women have more body fat than men, are women often colder? No one really knows for sure, but there are theories. One is that when it is cold out, warm blood goes to our core, and our layer of fat keeps it there more effectively than for men, but it also keeps the heat from coming to the surface of our skin.

Eating salty food can raise your blood pressure. That's the latest research in a debate that has gone back and forth for decades. In a study of 410 people, half of whom ate a regular American diet and half who ate a low-fat, vegetable-heavy diet, those eating the lowest amount of salt had the lowest blood pressure, no matter which diet they were on. And the lower the blood pressure, the lower the risk for stroke and heart disease.

Over 60 percent of women—but only 27 percent of men—believe that "the way to a partner's heart is through the stomach."

Klutzy Beyond Belief

Statistic keepers tell us that four thousand Americans injure themselves with pillows each year and six thousand hurt ourselves with blankets. The nature of the injuries is unclear.

And what about the three thousand of us who get hurt by our room deodorizers?

Or the eight thousand who are injured by musical instruments?

If you live in the United States, you will probably walk about 50,000 miles in your lifetime. And you will do some predictable damage to your shoes. Those in the know claim that the shoe on

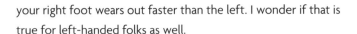

your right foot wears out faster than the left. I wonder if that is true for left-handed folks as well.

Anthropologists tell us that folks all around the world recognize the following facial expressions: anger, sadness, fear, happiness, surprise, and disgust.

Do you work in an office without walls? It may look great, but study after study has shown that workers are more stressed and less motivated in cubicles than in offices with walls and doors, no matter how tiny.

You Think the No-Smoking Policy in California Is Tough?

Ancient Turks caught inhaling tobacco were killed; Russians under the czars had their noses slit, then were whipped and exiled to Siberia.

Hitting the Gym

A study by Penn State University discovered that fatigue is the reason given by 70 percent of folks who fail to exercise regularly. But the truth is that exercise is just what we need to feel good—increased blood flow from exercise oxygenates the body and makes you feel more energized.

Exercise is such an energy booster that if you have trouble sleeping, experts recommend exercising at least five hours before going to bed.

"So far, I've always kept my diet secret, but now I might as well tell everyone what it is: lots of grapefruit throughout the day and plenty of virile young men at night."

—Angie Dickinson

Researchers at the University of Georgia recently discovered that exercise reduces anxiety better than resting.

Scientists at Arizona State University studied the effects of different kinds of exercise on the moods of folks sixty-two and older. By far, weight training worked the best.

Having trouble with an exercise routine? Studies have shown that women who work out in the morning have less stress and feel more content than those who don't. They are more likely to stick to an exercise routine than those who work out in the afternoon or evening—75 percent of those doing some aerobic activity in the a.m. were still doing it a year later, compared to only 50 percent of afternoon exercisers and 25 percent of evening "work-outers." If you do try a morning, eat a little something before you begin and then a regular breakfast afterwards.

Tennis players beware: women who play sports that require pivoting from the knee are at greater risk of knee injury than men. To reduce your chances, do weight training on your legs.

Women who play team sports are happier with their bodies than those of us who do not. So say researchers at the University of Florida at Gainesville.

Initially a human embryo looks most like a fish. At four weeks, it has slits near its neck that resemble gills. At six weeks, it sports a fishlike tail as well as arms and legs. As gestation continues, these disappear.

You are born with more than 800 bones in your body. But by the time you reach adulthood, you have only 360. Some have fallen out (your baby teeth) and others have fused, including your skull bones.

Treat That Brain Right

The human body is composed of about ten trillion cells. On any given day, three billion of those cells die and are replaced. The exception? Your brain. Its cells are finite. Once they die, they are gone forever.

Energy and Happiness Boosters

Researchers claim that twenty-four million women battle depression every year and that 74 percent could get relief in as short a time as a week by taking 200 mg of DLPA per day. DLPA is a combination of amino acids found in peas, lentils, and other protein-rich foods that is known to elevate blood levels of norepinephrine and the body's other natural mood elevators.

Regularly eating tuna, salmon, and other fish high in omega-3 fatty acids relieves depression in studies done by the National Institutes of Health (NIH). The reason? They increase levels of serotonin in the blood, which helps to increase calm and a sense of well-being. "The brain is essentially made of fat," explains Dr. Joseph Hibbeln of the NIH. "Some of the fats that are necessary for proper brain functioning cannot be manufactured by the body. They must be obtained in the diet."

Gingko biloba is an herb that is known for improving memory, but studies have indicated that it's a great antianxiety agent as well. According to Harold H. Bloomfield, MD, author of *Healing Anxiety with Herbs*, 120 to 180 mg a day lowers anxiety by as much as 79 percent.

Do you crave carbohydrates? Whole grain breads and cereals are thought to aid in making us feel calm and happy because they help deliver tryptophan, an amino acid, to the brain. Tryptophan increases the levels of serotonin, that magical chemical that makes us feel good.

One theory as to why so many of us women are dragging around and feeling listless is that we are all suffering from B complex vitamin deficiency. In *Natural Energy Boosters*, Carlson Wade suggests that the best and quickest way to replenish our store of B-vitamins is with brewer's yeast. He claims a shot of brewer's yeast when you're feeling low will beat tiredness, increase energy, and help resist depression.

Researchers have discovered that smiling is so powerful a happiness booster that our mood improves any time we turn up the corners of our mouth—even if it is only to hold a pen between our teeth.

Chamomile has long been considered an antidepressant as well as a mild sleep aid.

Laughing is good for you—it increases good hormones and decreases bad ones. Researchers at Cornell University have discovered that watching even five minutes of a funny movie made people feel happier.

Study after study shows that working women do more than their fair share of the housework; a study of 1,200 men and women by a researcher at Brown University found women to be doing 70 percent!

That same study, however, did something no one else had done before—it correlated happiness with the amount of work done and found, not surprisingly, that the bigger the woman's share, the more likely she was to feel depressed. And even more fascinating was that the amount of time a woman spent on housework wasn't significant; what mattered to her happiness was that the work, however long it took, be equally divided.

Women who were happiest did no more than 46 percent (while their spouses did about the same, and kids and hired help picked up the slack).

Research at Cornell University found that volunteering increases a person's energy, sense of mastery over life (a measure of happiness), and self-esteem.

Studies show that making your bed in the morning can keep depression away, but you may want to wait a couple hours before taking care of that daily task. Since 2006, research has demonstrated that if you allow the imperceptible perspiration in the bed to dry by exposing the interior of it to air and light, it significantly decreases the levels of tiny dust mites making it their home.

A new coenzyme supplement is being touted as an energy booster: Enada NADH is found naturally in beef, fish, chicken, and turkey, but our bodies can process only a small amount from food. In studies, 31 percent of those who took NADH supplements felt perkier in two weeks and 71 percent ultimately felt more energetic.

Herbalists are singing the praises of an energy booster—Arctic root (Latin name *Rhodiola rosea*), which is said to increase energy four times better than ginseng.

Did you know that a moderate amount of sunlight, particularly morning sun, is good for you? Many of us are aware that our bodies create vitamin D from sunlight, but recent research shows that a half hour of sun in the morning will elevate our mood and energy. That's because, according to Norma Rosenthal, MD, author of *Winter Blues*, "Sunlight increases the production of serotonin and norepinephrine," which are natural uppers. And why morning light? "In the morning," says the good doctor, "the eyes are most sensitive to the mood-altering effects of light."

Color therapy is the use of colors to promote emotional well-being. It has been used throughout history to influence moods, and in recent decades, psychologists have devised tests to demonstrate that color does influence how we feel (and even how fast we eat—hence the bright colors of fast-food restaurants designed to get you out the door quickly). For example, the Blackfriars Lodge in London, which was painted black, was known for a high suicide rate. When the building was painted green, the rate dropped by one-third. So, to enhance happiness, avoid black, violet, and blue (as all can increase depression).

What colors should you surround yourself with? According to color therapists: orange. Orange promotes optimism, enthusiasm, and happiness. Red also can help overcome depression but is not recommended for overly excitable personalities.

The more friends you have, the better you'll be protected from stress-related illnesses. In a study at Penn State University, researcher Mark Roy found that blood pressure rises when faced with stressors such as divorce, moving, job loss (setting the stage for heart disease). But the more friends a subject had, the lower their blood pressure.

According to Harvard University Professor Arthur Barsky, in national surveys, 46 percent of people say that "good health" is the greatest source of happiness, scoring higher than "great wealth" and "personal satisfaction from accomplishments."

The average woman will be sick about one-sixth of her lifetime (which must take into account the illnesses of old age, or it would be lower).

Vegetarians are generally 10 percent leaner than meat eaters and are half as likely to have high blood pressure.

According to research at the National Institute of Mental Health, drinking four cups of coffee a day can elevate your stress hormones and blood pressure by as much as 32 percent. They claim that women with full-blown anxiety have cured themselves without drugs simply by eliminating caffeine.

A recent study by the University of Michigan shows that dwelling on what's making us mad only increases the intensity of the feeling. Their suggestion: distract yourself.

As we age, we stop growing, with the exception of our ears—they keep growing and growing. (I thought noses did too.) And of course our girth can continue to grow as well if we don't cut down on our caloric intake and increase our exercise.

Women suffer from constipation more than men and tend to get sick more often in general. We go to doctors 50 percent more often and see dentists 30 percent more often.

Hairy Info

How much hair do you have on your body? Scientists put it at about five million hairs, many of them so fine you can hardly see them.

All your hair grows—body hair to about a half inch, at which point it goes dormant. Head hair grows about a half inch a month for two to six years (faster in warm weather and slower in cold; that's counterintuitive, I must say) before becoming dormant. At any given moment, 10 percent of your hair is dormant.

Each individual hair on your head stays dormant for about three months and then is shed when a new hair starts growing there. You lose about a hundred hairs a day.

If you never cut your hair, it would be around three feet long, although there are people whose hair has gotten a lot longer. A woman in New England has hair that is ten feet long.

Blondes have more hair than the rest of us; redheads have the least.

Hair grows faster at night than during the day and grows the most rapidly between the ages of sixteen and twenty-four!

All of us are slightly taller in the morning than at night because the disks between our spines expand a bit while we are lying down and get compressed during the day due to the pull of gravity.

Can't remember the name of someone you don't like? It may be on purpose. Scientists at the University of Oregon in Eugene found that they could cause the likelihood of remembering something to be reduced by 10 percent by telling people to forget it. That demonstrates that we selectively forget— and what better to forget than something we don't want to remember?

Some of us are genetically more suited to high-stress jobs than others. Researchers at Duke University have discovered that those with certain genes react more strongly to stress, as measured by elevation in blood pressure, than those with other types of genetic makeup.

According to the Center for Disease Control and Prevention in Atlanta, sudden cardiac death is on the rise for women age fifteen to thirty-four—it went up 30 percent from 1989 to 1996. They suspect lack of exercise and obesity are the main factors involved.

Between ages thirty and eighty, we lose 64 percent of our taste buds. However, taste tends to outlast all the other senses.

Prescreening Yourself

We all know about giving ourselves breast exams to detect breast cancer. But there are other self-tests we can easily try. Don't panic if something seems wrong; just go check it out with your doctor.

Many women suffer from anemia. With your forefinger, press on your thumbnail so that it turns whitish underneath. When you release the pressure, does the nail bed turn pink again? It if stays pale, you may be anemic.

Yellowish nails are usually a sign of a fungal infection, but they could be an indication of a disease of the liver, thyroid, kidney, or other vital system.

Check your earlobes twice a year for a diagonal crease. It could be that you are at increased risk for a heart attack. Don't panic if your ears have a vertical crease—that is most always caused by wearing heavy earrings.

Do you have raised yellow patches on your upper eyelids? It could be a sign of high cholesterol.

Look at the whites of your eyes. If they are even a bit yellow, have your liver function checked.

Why Is Life So Unfair?

Scientists inform us that on average, women's skin ages ten years faster than men's.

Before air travel, it used to take four months for a strain of the flu to make it around the world. Today it's four days.

If you live an average life span, you will be alive 26,280 days.

Oh, to Sleep

Experts say one in four people have trouble sleeping, at least occasionally, and the National Commission on Sleep Disorders estimates that folks spend sixteen billion dollars a year trying to sleep.

One study suggests that women who are sleep deprived tend to eat more fast food and have more road rage than they do when they sleep well.

Seventy-two percent of men surveyed say they sleep better on the couch than in bed with their mates.

Two sisters in France spent ten months out of every year in bed for forty-eight years.

Sixty-four percent of women sleep on the left side of the bed.

Men are three times as likely to sleep in the nude as are women.

Sleeping pills were first invented by Celsus, a Roman, in the first century BC. He put mandrake and henbane into pills for insomniacs.

Our biological clocks are so regulated by changes in light and dark that according to Margaret Moline, director of the Sleep-Wake Disorders Center at the New York Hospital, even fifteen minutes of bright light can inhibit your ability to go to sleep.

Studies have shown that waking up to an alarm clock interrupts your body's natural circadian rhythms, which can negatively affect your mood for the rest of the day. Before falling asleep, if you envision the time you want to wake up, most people will wake within a few minutes of the envisioned time, leading researchers to speculate that our biological clocks are in communication with our subconscious minds.

There is tremendous variation in how much sleep people need. Some of us need ten hours, others much less. The average is eight, although scientists once studied a woman in her seventies who slept no more than one hour a night and was completely healthy. Her record for staying awake was fifty-six hours, and even then she only slept for one and a half hours after that, feeling just dandy.

To break the world record, a woman in England went without sleep for 449 hours, or almost nineteen days. She was in a rocking chair the whole time.

Women are twice as more likely than men to report having nightmares.

Here's an easy way to figure out if you are overweight: a woman's waist should be no more than thirty-three inches, or you are at risk for health problems.

Those in the know tell us that fried foods, chocolate, pizza, and other such items do not cause acne. (They do cause other problems, though.)

Eight out of every ten of us will have acne at some point in our lives, and 89 percent of teenage girls say it is one of their biggest worries.

We always hear the name of British doctor Alexander Fleming when we learn about the discovery of penicillin. But he could not have done it without Anne Miller. It was 1942. Anne was near death from a bacterial infection in a hospital in Connecticut. Having nothing to lose, she agreed to try Fleming's drug, which had never been tested in the United States. She was given an injection and within twenty-four hours was miraculously better. The rest is medical history.

CHAPTER 3

Ladies' Matters of Love

According to *Longevity* magazine, more than 50 percent of married men and women do not consider their spouse their best-ever lover.

Pornography Can Be Bad for Your Sex Life

After looking at nude photos in *Playboy* and other men's magazines, both men and women feel their mates are less attractive and report that they feel less in love.

What are the most romantic things you can do? When asked, people's first choice is lying in front of a fireplace, followed by taking a shower together and walking on the beach.

According to another study, 80 percent of us think a vacation is the best way to rekindle romance.

Not a Good Start

Stories of wedding ceremonies gone awry:

- They had just cut the ceremonial piece of cake when a French bride took the frosting-covered knife and stabbed her spouse.

- A mother of the groom at a wedding in England couldn't hold her tongue when the minister asked if anyone knew any reason the couple should not be wed, shouting that the bride was a tramp who was not good enough for her son. She had to be removed by police.

- A best man stood to the left of the groom, rather than the right, and ended up married to the bride at an Irish wedding in the 1920s. It was only discovered when the priest asked the best man to sign the register and the real groom announced that he thought he was supposed to do it. There had to be a second ceremony.

- The minister tripped over a Bible, falling, gashing his head, and breaking his foot at an English wedding in 1996. But he insisted on going on with the ceremony before seeking medical care—and so he did, with blood pouring down his face.

- In 1986, a happy couple were about to drive away on their honeymoon when they discovered their car had been stolen.

- Many people have been known to faint during their weddings. But one English bride holds the record for longest swoon—it took twenty minutes to revive her.

- Pity poor Mrs. Cullen of Arkansas. Her husband dropped dead of a heart attack driving away on their honeymoon. Later she discovered that the best man had also had a heart attack that night and died.

In 1797, a bride in Birmingham, England, got married stark naked. No, she wasn't a confirmed nudist. She did it because there was a belief at the time that if a woman of means married a man with debts, his creditors would not be able to come after her for the money owed if she married in the nude.

According to Rutgers University National Marriage Project, 60 percent of American women and 65 percent of American men report that they are involved in "very happy" marriages. Marriages may be happier, but fewer and fewer Americans are tying the knot; only 67 percent of women and 66 percent of men aged thirty-five to forty-four were married in 2005, down from 81 percent of females and 84 percent of males in 1980, and these numbers are continuing to decline—in 2017, only 55 percent of all American adults were married.

Can baseball save your marriage? A study out of the Denver University reported that the divorce rate is 28 percent lower in cities with major league baseball teams than in those without.

How about bathing suit weather? It has been reported that the divorce rate among Americans is higher in those areas with more warm weather days, and lower in colder areas. Draw a line along the midsection of the United States, and you'll find that less than half the divorces occur in the far denser northern half of the country.

How about higher education? Statisticians inform us that women who complete sixteen or more years of school are less likely to divorce their first husbands.

May—December Unions

Ruth and Kevin Kember married when she was ninety-three and he was twenty-eight.

Octavio Gullen and Adriana Martinez were engaged for sixty-seven years before they finally tied the knot.

Scientists tell us that because of hormones, we are at our sexual peaks in the morning. Nature planned it that way so the caveman would plant his seed before he went out in search of food in case he didn't come back.

British women told pollsters that they would rather give up having sex than having to abstain from chocolate.

"When people ask me how we've lived past a hundred, say, 'Honey, we were never married. We never had husbands to worry us to death.' "

—Bessie Delany, on why she and her sister lived so long

Looking for someone of the opposite sex? Women should go to Alaska, where the largest concentration of men are, and men should move to Washington, DC, where women outnumber men the most.

Famous Folks on Wedded Bliss

If love means never having to say you're sorry, then marriage means always having to say everything twice."

—Estelle Getty, geriatric Golden Girl

"Gettin' married is a lot like getting into a tub of hot water. After you get used to it, it ain't so hot."

—Minnie Pearl

"I've only slept with men I've been married to. How many women can make that claim?"

—Elizabeth Taylor

"Separate bedrooms
and separate
bathrooms."

—Bette Davis, on the secret of a
good marriage

The Taj Mahal was built in the seventeenth century by Shah Jahan at the deathbed request of his wife Mumtaz Mahal (Ornament of the Palace) as an appropriate resting place for her. Deeply in love, the grief-stricken monarch ordered the construction of the mausoleum, which took over two decades and 20,000 jewelers, masons, and calligraphers to construct. As soon as the work was completed, the Shah ordered a companion one in black marble for himself.

A great love story, right? Well, it turns out that Mumtaz was an Islamic fanatic who before her death insisted that the Shah, a live-and-let-live kind of guy, destroy the Christian city of Hoogly and sell its people into slavery (except for the priests, who were killed by having elephants trample them). Perhaps he should have loved her less.

Ultimately, he was deposed by his son, who was angered over the expense of the Taj Mahal and his father's never-completed final resting place. Son sent Dad to prison, where he sat for eight years, staring at the monument he had created. It wasn't such a bad life; he brought his harem with him. And, despite mourning for his deceased wife, he wasn't averse to having fun. Reputedly the cause of his death at seventy-four was from overdoing it with aphrodisiacs.

Kissing Uncovered

Ancient Romans kissed someone on the mouth or eyes as a greeting.

Ancients also kissed a hand, foot, or the ground a person walked on as a sign of respect.

Some theorize that kissing came from people putting their faces close together and exchanging breaths to symbolize union.

The fancy word for what you are doing when you kiss is *osculation*.

The longest lip lock on screen was between Regis Toomey and Jane Wyman in *You're in the Army Now*. It was three minutes and fifteen seconds.

You burn twenty-six calories in a one-minute kiss.

The worst kiss, according to the book *The Best of the World's Worst*, was one between Samuel Pepys and Catherine de Valois, wife of Henry V of England, for when the kiss happened, she was dead. Long dead—she had been disentombed by her grandson during his renovation of Westminster Abbey and remained above ground for two centuries. At some point as she lay there, Pepys kissed her, saying that he had always wanted to kiss a queen.

How did an *x* get to mean a kiss at the end of a letter? The tradition comes from the Middle Ages, when illiterate folks would sign an x for their name and then kiss it as proof of their sincerity.

Kissing died out during the bubonic plague of the fifteenth century. Folks were too afraid of dying to lock lips.

Finally, I've found where the notion of French kissing originated: It comes from the Maraîchins, who lived in France, spoke their own unique dialect of Poitevin, and practiced this kind of deep kissing.

According to the *New England Journal of Medicine*, the best cure for menstrual cramps is sex.

During the Victorian era, the polite word for intercourse was "flourish."

Contemplating Condoms

Condoms have been around for thousands of centuries. The ancient Chinese constructed them from silk paper that had been oiled, but Roman soldiers, known for their brutality, were said to have made them from the bodies of their foes.

In the 1700s, people were using animal intestines that went through an elaborate process of cleaning, drying, and oiling. That method was pioneered in the 1600s by a Frenchman, Conton, who used lamb intestines to construct the shields for Charles II, who was quite promiscuous and feared syphilis. It is Conton who lent his name to the devices.

Or maybe not. Another source tells me that they were first brought into use in the West in the 1500s by Gabriel Fallopius, who also "discovered" fallopian tubes.

Still another says no one knows who first thought of such a thing.

Condoms got the nickname "rubbers" in the 1850s, when they began being made from that sturdy substance. They were considered reusable, after washing.

Latex condoms did not become widely available until the 1930s.

Five billion condoms are sold worldwide every year.

Condoms come in all sorts of colors and textures. But don't look for any green ones in Islamic nations; they are generally forbidden because green is considered a holy color.

Speaking of contraceptives, the notion of using something to control pregnancy was first thought of by the Egyptians in 2000 BC.

Nowadays, fully 50 percent of couples worldwide use some form of birth control. The leading contraceptive used in the United States in 2002 was the pill, used by 11.6 million women; the second most common method was female sterilization, used by 10.3 million women. The condom was the third most popular.

Ninon de Lenclos is considered the last of the great French courtesans of the 1600s. She slept with five thousand men, many of whom came from the Parisian elite. She once charged Cardinal Richelieu 50,000 crowns to spend an evening with her. When she was sixty-five, a young soldier smitten with her begged her to sleep with him. She refused, but he would not take no for an answer. Finally, she told him the reason—he was her son. Stunned, he fell on his sword and died. Ninon herself died at eighty-five, with lovers all the while.

Another famous lady of the night was a Spaniard known as La Belle Otero, who lived until the ripe old age of ninety-seven and claimed to have made twenty-five million dollars plying her trade. She died penniless, though, because she was a compulsive gambler.

The word *orchid* comes from the Greek word *orkhis*, meaning "testicle," because its roots reminded botanists of that male appendage. This may also have been the origin of the belief that orchids are aphrodisiacs.

Know any men suffering from erotomonomania? That's a psychological condition in which a man believes, despite evidence to the contrary, that women are desperate to sleep with him.

Take That

When one woman discovered her wealthy husband had a girlfriend shacked up in an apartment he was paying for, she raided the wine cellar and gave away seventy bottles of his most expensive wine.

Told to clear out by a man about to leave on a long business trip, the girlfriend calmly agreed. When he returned days later to his London apartment, she was indeed gone. But the phone was off the hook. The man didn't think anything of it—until he got that month's phone bill—for $2,500! The woman had called the number in the United States that used to automatically tell the time, and it had stayed engaged the whole time he was gone.

Then there's the Hollywood tale that the wife of a Hollywood producer, distraught over his dalliance with a nubile actress, bathed in caviar to rejuvenate her looks. The cost of the caviar appeared on his credit card, of course.

Granted, this one was not on purpose: Distraught over her husband's announcement that he was leaving her, a Czech housewife threw herself out the window. She survived because her fall was broken by landing on...her husband, who died immediately.

In general, men, it's not nice to get a woman mad at you. While it's true women kill less often than men, female murderers are five times more likely to kill a man than a woman. And it's usually someone she knows well.

"I'm not upset about my divorce. I'm only upset I'm not a widow."

—Roseanne Barr, after divorcing Tom Arnold

Murderous Mrs.

In 1968 during a telecast of the Miss America pageant, Peggy Bush killed her lawyer husband after he yelled at their fourteen-year-old daughter about the bills she'd been running up at the country club. At her trial, she testified that he had been swearing at her, although she could not say the words and used the initials "GD" and "SOB" instead—and that she thought the weapon was a "popgun;"—oops, it was a .22! In record time (three minutes), the jury declared her not guilty.

The more comfortable you are with your spouse, the less you will look at him or her when you are speaking. So say scientists, who claim it's because if you are unsure of the other person's reaction, you will be monitoring their facial expressions as you speak. If you feel comfortable, you don't have to watch them.

Have a disappointing sexual encounter? Most men will say it's their partner's fault. What about women? They blame themselves, of course.

Harassed Husbands

Here are some official reasons men have given for divorcing:

- His wife told him that he would have to cook his own dinner that night.
- She "served pea soup for breakfast and dinner...and packed his lunch with pea sandwiches."
- His wife "beat him whenever he removed onions from his hamburger without first asking for permission."

- She "wore earplugs whenever his mother came to visit."

- She dressed up as a ghost to scare away his mother.

Phryne, the most famous of the *hetairae* (high-class ancient call girls) of BC Greece, was put on trial for corrupting the morals of Athens' male citizenry. In her defense, she bared her breasts, at which point the judges declared her a goddess and she was set free.

The University of Florida College of Journalism did a survey of how often the subject of sex was covered in major magazines in one year. In men's magazines, the percentage was 66; in women's, 72.

Striptease was first practiced (publicly, at least) by an artist's model named Mona, who spontaneously flung her clothes off during the 1893 Four Arts Ball at the Moulin Rouge in Paris. She was fined a hundred francs, which then caused a riot during which students stormed police headquarters to protest her fine. The following year, a Parisian dancer named Yvette did the first staged striptease at the Divan Fayouan Music Hall.

An Indian sexologist counted 529 positions for sexual intercourse.

And a book, *The Female Member*, informs us that there are 640 nicknames for female genitals, twice as many as there are for the male member.

Ninety percent of couples in their sixties and 80 percent in their seventies have active sex lives.

However, American couples are reported to have sex a mere eighty-five times a year. Only the Japanese, Chinese, and Nigerians have less sex.

"A man when he is making up to anybody can be cordial and gallant and full of little attentions and altogether charming. But when a man is really in love he can't help looking like a sheep."

—Agatha Christie

A young woman in Germany, Emmie Marie Jones, gave birth to a daughter nine months after the bombardment of the Allies in Germany. Nothing necessarily out of the ordinary there— except that she insisted that she was a virgin. Neighbors and scientists snickered, until finally in 1955, scientists in England did genetic testing and discovered that Emmie and her daughter were genetically identical twins. Did the shock of the bombing cause parthenogenesis, the splitting of the egg without being fertilized? That's the only explanation they could come up with.

More babies are born in September than in any other month of the year. Whether that's due to the cold weather or the holiday season nine months before is unclear.

The first chastity belt appeared on a woman in Italy in the 1300s. But Homer gets the blame for the initial idea. In the *Odyssey*, Aphrodite's sweetie, Hephaistos, put her into a girdle as punishment for fooling around on him.

Here's another sexual statistic: By age eighteen, 55 percent of both male and female teenagers have had premarital sex. But twenty years ago, twice as many males had tried it out by that age as females.

Teens Who Wish They'd Said No

In a recent study, 73 percent of twelve- to fourteen-year-olds who were sexually active wished they had waited until they were older; so did 58 percent of fifteen- to seventeen-year-olds.

Seven percent of schools in the United States offer no sex education, and 35 percent do not allow educators to discuss birth control or safe sex. 63 percent of schools do not teach students how to use a condom.

When parents pay attention, sex education works better. That's the result of a study that found that parents who help out with sex-ed homework have children who participate less in risky sexual behavior compared to kids of parents who were nonparticipatory.

Oops!

An Italian couple on their honeymoon decided to film their wedding night. But when they hooked up the VCR, something went wrong and their activities were broadcast to everyone in their apartment building who had their TVs on.

A hotel in Chicago had a great idea—send a thank-you letter to the 1,200 folks who had stayed at their hotel that past year. There was only one problem: They accidentally sent the letter instead to 1,200 people who never had been to the hotel. They discovered their error when they got hundreds of phone calls from irate people who suddenly were being accused of infidelity by their mates, including one from a pregnant lady who said her husband was convinced by their letter that the baby wasn't his.

Other Wedding Tidbits

In many cultures of old, the happy couple had to make love for the first time in the presence of witnesses who could attest to the consummation of the marriage. Most of us don't do that anymore, but we do have a vestige of that practice—the wedding kiss.

The practice of the bridal party honking their horns as they drive away comes from the notion that loud noises scare off evil spirits.

Most of us spend around a hundred dollars for a wedding present.

Just like throwing rice, the eating of the wedding cake was meant to promote fertility.

The average price of a wedding in the United States in the year 2005 was $30,000.

Another way to look at what weddings typically cost is: the average person spends half of the typical worker's annual salary to get wed and three years' salary to get divorced (including the settlement itself).

Where did the garter come from? Originally the guests at European weddings would accompany the couple into the bridal bedroom and pull off their stockings for them and toss them about. If you hit the bride or groom with a garter and you were a member of the opposite sex, it was believed you would be the next to get married.

Ancient Roman weddings always had a person whose job it was to tell dirty jokes, to turn the attention of possibly evil gods away from the happy couple. That practice has morphed into the best man's speech.

Where did we get the phrase "tying the knot"? No one knows for sure, but cultures around the world use some form of tying during the wedding ceremony to symbolize the union expressed in marriage. In Hindu ceremonies, the groom places a ribbon around the bride's neck and ties a knot in it. In European weddings, the wedding couple has their wrists tied together. And thousands of years ago in Carthage, the couple's thumbs were tied together.

Slaves in the United States were not permitted to marry, so couples would unite by the practice of jumping over a broom handle, which stood for the jump from single to married life.

A recent long-range study has found that whereas gay and lesbian couples face more external stressors on their relationships because of prejudice, they actually tend to have better communication skills than heterosexual couples and use fewer hostile tactics during fights.

In the 1920s and '30s, it was easy to get a divorce in Russia. You didn't even have to inform your spouse. All you had to do was send a notification to the registrar's office and they would send a postcard in the mail to your intended ex. Bingo, you are divorced.

A man in California kept calling the police to complain that the woman next door was harassing him. But they could never catch her doing anything. Finally, one Easter, the man called again, and the police rushed over—to find the woman completely naked and covered in chocolate, hopping on his lawn, trying to woo him as a chocolate Easter bunny.

Cosmopolitan once did a survey of men's feelings about sex that revealed all manner of fascinating facts:

- 44 percent of men don't like it when women jump up after making love and put their clothes on.

- 62 percent prefer being the giver, if they had to choose.

- 71 percent think hairy legs on ladies are a turn-off, and that goes up to 77 percent when it comes to armpits.

- Men are most turned on by women saying what they want in bed—88 percent, a percentage that was much higher than for any other possible choice.

- 40 percent prefer their females in thongs rather than bikinis. And 53 percent love to see women in lacy bras.

- Men are evenly divided between which is sexier when bared in a top—breasts or belly buttons.

- Most are tolerant of a woman's right to choose—78 percent said they would not dump a woman for refusing to have oral sex.

Of course, men have concerns during sex as well:

- 53 percent are afraid of not satisfying their partners. If a woman is totally quiet, 54 percent are concerned they are not doing something right.

- The body part they worry the most about not being pleasing to their partners is their stomachs—30 percent of men worry about that. Only 16 percent are concerned about penis size.

According to one survey, nearly 59 percent of women did not enjoy their first sexual encounter. What percentage of men say the same thing? Four.

Women who enjoy sex the most tend to be more educated, childless, and making more money than other women.

On average, it takes five and a half months of unprotected sex to get pregnant. (On purpose, that is.)

Before marrying, the average woman has had four sex partners or fewer; the average man has had ten.

Men stand closer to women in elevators than they do other men. Women exhibit no gender preferences. Either sex will stand closer if the other person smiles.

A study in the *Journal of Health and Social Behavior* demonstrated that for teens, falling in love leads to more depression, delinquency, and alcohol use than not.

In Puritan New England, fully dressed unmarried couples were sent to bed to do their courting because there was no money for heating the living room. A wooden board called a bundling board was placed between them to prevent hanky-panky. But it must not have worked very well, because the rate of illegitimate births soared.

A *Playboy* survey of 100,000 people found that men are more likely to commit adultery the more money they make. For men earning more than $60,000, it's 70 percent.

If you are having an affair, chances are it is with a friend or coworker, with an old flame coming in third as a possibility.

The Not Fun Side

Please note: These next few items contain data on sexual assaults and other sexual victimization. Please consider skipping down to the next chapter if reading them is likely to cause you undue discomfort.

As many as one in six women may have been victims of sexual abuse by a family member or friend.

A woman is sexually assaulted somewhere in the United States every two and a half minutes.

Fifty-eight percent of all rapes happen at night, and July is the month during which the most forcible rapes occur.

According to the World Health Organization, more than 130 million women around the world have been genitally mutilated.

Streetwalkers in ancient Rome had to dye their hair yellow (they used saffron) and wear short skirts to differentiate themselves from proper Roman matrons.

One of the most infamous nymphomaniacs was Valeria Messalina, wife of the Roman emperor Claudius. She turned one of the rooms of his palace into a whorehouse, charging just what the ladies in the street did. Once she bet the most famous prostitute of the time that she could have sex with more men in twenty-four hours than the other woman could. And she did win—by twenty-five men!

Another famous lover of sex, Catherine the Great was rumored to have kept a stable of women "testers" to sleep with men before she did to ensure they were disease-free and worth her time in terms of technique.

You've heard, of course, of the red-light district, but in China in the Tang dynasty, whorehouses were distinguished by a blue lantern in the window and so, of course, were called blue houses (leading eventually to the practice of calling pornographic films "blue movies").

The Lowdown on the World's Oldest Profession

Only 20 percent of full-contact sex workers are streetwalkers.

At least one-fourth of prostitutes were sexually abused as kids.

When the United States was being colonized, there was a great shortage of women. To solve the problem, King Louis XV sent the entire population of female prostitutes and criminals in his jail to New Orleans. England followed suit by sending their incarcerated women to the thirteen colonies.

CHAPTER 4

In the Ladies' Room

Toilets in various forms have been around for thousands of years. The very first indoor place to do your business was created on the islands off the coast of Scotland in 2800 BC. Folks would squat over pits, and drains would take waste away. The first seated toilet, it is claimed, was created in Pakistan thousands of years ago. And the ancient Cretans invented a mechanism by which their toilets flushed.

Unfortunately, like so many other good Eastern ideas, particularly about cleanliness, the knowledge was lost to Europe during the Middle Ages and didn't resurface until the sixteenth century (even Versailles was built without toilets). Queen Elizabeth I had one made for her in 1596. But the ancestor of the toilet as we now know it was patented by an Englishman, Alexander Cumming, in 1775.

Toilet paper was a hard sell when it was first introduced in the mid-1800s. Frugal Americans used pages of newsprint for free— why should they pay for something new, they reasoned. Those in Britain under the spell of Queen Victoria were too uptight to purchase it. As indoor toilets caught on, however, so did the special paper.

The Chinese had the idea for toilet paper ages ago—for royalty only, though. Theirs was even scented! For centuries, folks everywhere else in the world had to make do with sticks, hay, and leaves (except for French royalty in the seventeenth century—they used lace and soft wool). Colonial Americans employed corn cobs.

Bidets (from the French word for "pony") were invented in France, where the noblewomen of Versailles took to them instantly. Theirs were enclosed in small, wooden, highly decorated, freestanding cabinets. Marie Antoinette loved hers so much that she insisted on bringing it with her when she was imprisoned prior to her execution.

In the United States, we somehow got the idea that bidets are naughty. However, they were invented to *conserve* water, allowing folks to clean their privates with a minimum amount of liquid needed. Fewer and fewer French homes have them these days; the country with the most bidets now is Japan.

The Scoop on Soap

Soap is thousands of years old, first used by Hittites, Sumerians, and Phoenicians. It has even been found in the ruins of Pompeii. It was not widely employed in the West, however, until physicians realized it could help stop the spread of bacterial disease.

As early as AD 1, soap makers were adding perfumes and dyes to make their products look and smell better. Even now, though, no matter what the price, scent, or other ingredients, the basis of most soap is fat and grease mixed with lye.

Soap only works on greasy dirt. If you have plain garden dirt on you, water and 'elbow grease' will do just fine. But because water can't dissolve grease, water alone can't get rid of greasy dirt; only soap or detergent can. Soap is a tricky substance chemically. One side of its molecules attracts grease, so it clings to it; the other side attracts water. Soap molecules therefore attract both dirt and water, so when you rinse and dry yourself off, the dirt is down the drain.

The Egyptians were nuts for cleanliness, bathing up to three times a day, removing body hair with pumice, and perfuming their whole bodies.

In the West, until relatively recently, bathing was seen as dangerous, something to be indulged in annually and only in warm weather. (Even in the late twentieth century, my grandmother, a stern woman originally from Ireland, prided herself on only washing her hair twice a year!) Naturally, folks were a bit ripe smelling when bath time rolled around; hence the popularity of strong perfumes. Wealthy folks and royalty would not only douse themselves but their clothes and shoes too. Queen Elizabeth I had her own special blend of perfume made exclusively for her from eight grains of must and sugar stirred into rosewater and damask water. The mixture simmered for five hours and was then cooled and strained.

Other women of the times would wear necklaces of scented beads that gave off a strong aroma; popular ones were made of rose petals cooked and hardened into balls that were then strung. And it didn't do to have stinky dogs, either; the ladies of Queen Elizabeth's court would rub scents into their lapdogs before taking them out to visit.

Bathing was so taboo in western Europe that Queen Elizabeth I was considered a cleanliness fanatic for bathing once a month.

Today, one in every three women sees a bath as a way to pamper herself, not just to get clean.

Indeed, we Westerners now pride ourselves on daily showers or baths and spend a fortune on fancy soaps and shampoos. As you look at the list of ingredients in your shampoo, be aware that many of them are pure marketing gimmicks. Take, for example, vitamins. Since hair is dead, putting vitamins on it does absolutely nothing.

Bathrooms can be dangerous places. Of course the biggest risk is to children, who can die in the tub. Surprisingly, most of the risk to kids comes from scalding, not drowning.

And women (as well as men) with long hair, beware. A few women do die each year when their hair gets caught in a hot-tub suction drain.

If You Are Happy with Your Hair, Thank John Breck

Originally, people would wash their hair as well as their bodies with soap. But as anyone who has tried it in an emergency knows, soap does not wash completely out of hair, making it very stringy. As early as the 1800s, inventors were trying to find something better, and in continental Europe they began to use detergent, which did rinse out thoroughly. But the trend had not caught on in the United States or Great Britain.

Then in 1898, along came John Breck, a balding twenty-one-year-old who was very unhappy about his hair loss. Unable to find help, he began to study chemistry at Amherst College in Massachusetts in hopes of finding a baldness cure, eventually receiving a PhD. It was during his studies that he discovered the detergent trick the Europeans were using. In 1929, he partnered with a beauty supply dealer and launched the John H. Breck Corporation, introducing shampoo to the American market.

In the 1930s, he was the first to introduce pH-balanced shampoo as well as shampoos specifically formulated for oily and dry hair. If you are old enough, perhaps you have seen his ad campaign that began in the '40s and ran for decades featuring "Breck Girls," white models with long flowing tresses.

Hair conditioner first came into popular usage a bit later. Fundamentally, it is a waxy, greasy, or plastic-like liquid that is used to coat your hair's jagged edges. When you wash your hair, the detergent strips the oils out and the jagged edges of your hair catch on one other, making snarls and causing breakage. Conditioner fills in the jagged spots, making hair easier to comb and giving it a softer feel.

The idea of putting perfumed oils or bath salts in a tub of water before soaking goes back to ancient Egypt. The Queen of Sheba received bath salts as a gift from King Solomon, while pundits claim that Cleopatra convinced Marc Antony to invade a certain area to keep her in bathing oils. (Given the fact that she was an astute political strategist, there were probably other reasons as well.)

For centuries, Indian fiancées bathed every day for a month in perfumed baths to prepare for their weddings.

And rumor has it that as long ago as three thousand years, wealthy women in Japan would bath in sake.

The ancient Greeks preferred bathing in cold water, believing it promoted good health. The Spartans, the toughest guys in the Greek world, went so far as to say it was effeminate to use hot water.

Why is the spigot on the right the cold water and the one on the left hot? Well, says the guy who wrote *Bathroom Stuff*, it's because most people are right-handed, and back in the days before hot water, the one and only spigot was placed on the right.

Bath towels come in every shade of the rainbow, but the bestselling ones are all in dark colors—wine, navy, and dark green. These three colors alone account for almost 80 percent of sales.

Americans prefer plushy, fluffy towels, Europeans thin ones with a waffle pattern.

Not for the Squeamish of Stomach

I finally found out why towels start smelling—when you dry yourself, dead skin comes off, which is the perfect medium for mildew.

The More the Merrier

In the Middle Ages, couples used to get married in the bathtub because water signified purity. The couple and their attendants would stand in a tub filled with water.

If you linger in the bathtub, chances are you will emerge as a wrinkled prune. That's because prolonged exposure to water causes skin's natural water repellent, keratin, to dissolve and the cells in the epidermis layer to absorb water and swell, causing puckering. Once you get out of the water, the cells go back to their normal size as the water evaporates and the puckers disappear.

Before the days of indoor plumbing, wealthy French women didn't like the idea of showing their bodies in public at the public bathhouses. So they would pay for horse-drawn bathtubs to come to them—complete with towels and hot water.

Humans have been cleaning their teeth since as early as 1.8 million years ago. Originally we used only toothpicks, which were once so popular that the ancient Chinese would wear them as necklaces. During the Renaissance, wealthy Europeans had them made in gold and strung on necklaces.

The precursor to the toothbrush was the chew stick. Mohammed increased their popularity by teaching that a chew and then a prayer were as good as seventy prayers by themselves.

The toothbrush as we know it, with bristles, was first made in the 1400s in China from hog hairs. Meanwhile, in Europe, people were wiping their teeth with rags until the late eighteenth century, when toothbrushes began to be widely used.

It's hard to believe that something so simple could have so many variations, but *Bathroom Stuff* says that there are more than three thousand patents for toothbrushes.

I Thought It Was Only Me

The average dental flosser uses 18 yards of floss per year; however, dentists recommend we use a foot and one-half per day, which would come to over 183 yards annually.

More than three million miles of dental floss are bought each year in North America. Then why do so few of us floss?

Historians tell us that toothpaste was first used about a thousand years ago by a Roman called Scibonius Largus. Where he got the idea is unclear, but he decided to mix honey, salt, and ground glass together and brush it onto his teeth with his finger. If you think that's bad, later on, Spaniards and Portuguese used human urine as toothpaste, dipping their toothbrushes liberally. It worked well because urine contains ammonia.

To combat bad breath, ancient Romans would drink perfume.

Researchers tell us that 87 percent of Americans claim to have been taught how to clean the bathroom (and the rest of the house) by their mothers, while 63 percent learned how to avoid cleaning from their fathers.

Mirror, Mirror

The ancient Egyptians were the first to have mirrors. Theirs were made of highly polished circles of copper or bronze.

Glass mirrors first came into use in the 1600s, when Venetian artisans perfected the art of blowing glass.

Mirrors ward off evil spirits—or so thought the ancient Chinese, who were convinced that spirits do not want to be seen in a looking glass.

👓 👓 👓

Women in the United States use more face cloths and sponges than women in other countries do and therefore have traditionally been heavier users of bar soap than shower gel. But when marketers figured this out, they began packaging shower gels with puffs and sponges and saw their sales soar by 40 percent.

Thirty percent of us avoid using public restrooms because of cleanliness concerns. So say the folks at Quilted Northern, who commissioned a survey on the subject. Those of us who are willing to use the facilities do take extra precautions. Over

40 percent use their feet to flush to avoid touching the toilet handle with their hand. And over half of us never sit on the seat, but hover instead.

The truth has come out. In this day of cellular telephones, about half of us surveyed owned up to talking on the phone while on the throne.

A guy from Wisconsin was once arrested for being in the women's bathroom at a mall. His reason, he explained, was that it was the best place he could think of to pick up women.

In 1997, 60 percent of Japanese households lacked a flush toilet.

The first bathtub didn't appear in the White House until 1851.

A recent survey discovered that many more men read on the toilet than women. It is not clear at all why that is. We gals might want to break down and make an exception for National Bathroom Reading Week, the second week of June.

"Water—the mighty,
the pure, the beautiful,
the unfathomable."

—Letitia Elizabeth Landon,
The Book of Beauty

CHAPTER 5

Ladies, Look at the Animal Kingdom

When someone talks about doing the lion's share of the work, they are definitely talking about the female lion. This rugged dame not only rears the babies alone but also does 90 percent of the hunting for the pride. The male's job is much easier—mating, roaring, and urinating to ward off nomad males.

Oopsie Doopsie

During the Middle Ages, the Catholic Church got it into its head that cats were the agents of the devil. So it ordered the extermination of all cats. For two hundred years, there were cat burnings and other forms of cat murder. If you tried to protect your puss, you could be burned at the stake as a witch. Consequently, the population of cats in Europe was decimated, which had an effect the church hadn't considered—the rat population, now unchecked, exploded. And so did the plague, which was spread by the fleas on rats. Ultimately, 75 percent of the population of Europe died in the plague. Cats' revenge, perhaps? Too late, the church saw the error of its ways and reversed its order, decreeing that good Christians must treat cats kindly.

Speaking of cats, if they'd had Dusty around during the Middle Ages, perhaps not as many folks would have died. Dusty was a Texas tabby cat who held the record for the most kittens—420, including one born when she was seventeen.

Texan Victoria Herberta loved her pig Priscilla so much that she even slept with her. But in 1984, the rest of the world came to love Priscilla, too, when she saved a boy from drowning by swimming out to him, getting him to hold onto her collar, and then bringing him to shore.

Got an Itch? Blame a Woman... Mosquito

Only female mosquitoes bite; they feed on blood. Male mosquitoes feed on rotting fruit and vegetables.

Only female spiders get to live to old age. Female tarantulas, for instance, may live up to twenty-five or beyond. Males only make it to ten, the mating age, for once the act is consummated, the female devours them. Black widows also kill their mates, which gives them their ferocious name. The venom from a black widow is fifteen times stronger than that of a rattlesnake.

The female Goliath tarantula can have a leg span as large as a dinner plate. Fortunately for spider-phobic residents of the United States, they live in South America.

Female spiders spin better webs than males do. All webs are amazing, though—the thread is so strong that if it were an inch in diameter, it would be stronger than an iron rope of the same diameter and capable of holding 74 tons.

Swans, storks, termites, vultures, pigeons, gorillas, beavers, penguins, and foxes are among the animals that mate for life. So do geese, who mourn when their partner dies.

The female praying mantis is also known for killing her mate, usually by biting his head off during the sex act (but his sex drive is so strong, say scientists, that he can keep on going, even sans head). Perhaps it's an accident—they have very bad eyesight and eat anything that moves, which can also include their babies, parents, and random visitors.

Cuttlefish have a whole different approach to childrearing. They mate and then both die; the offspring hatches on its own and fends for itself immediately.

The female sunfish holds the world's record for producing the most eggs at once: three hundred million at a shot.

Desert rats may have sex as frequently as 122 times per hour, while the multimammate rat has as many as 120 babies per year.

Armadillos always give birth to a litter of four—and each litter is either all male or all female. Wonder what that is about—incest protection perhaps?

Oysters are masters at sex change operations—they change their gender annually. Depending on water temperature and salinity, they spawn in either female or male form.

TV's Lassie led the good life—even to the point of having an air-conditioned kennel. Someone once estimated that during the life of the show, she (who was really a he—male collies being larger and more beautiful, or so thought producers) had leapt through 47 windows, caught 152 bad guys, rescued 73 other animals, and jumped onto 17 moving vehicles.

She Had on Her Traveling Shoes

A Russian cat named Murka lived with a woman who could no longer take care of her. So she gave Murka to her mother, who lived four hundred miles away. As soon as Murka got to the mother's house, she disappeared—only to resurface at her original owner's house a year later, filthy, starving, missing the end of her tail, and pregnant. Somehow she had found her way back home over four hundred miles.

🐝🐝🐝🐝🐝

Seahorses mate during the full moon. And they are great examples of role reversal—it is the male that bears the children. Mom releases eggs into a pouch on Dad's tummy, which he then fertilizes and carries to term. He's a busy dad too, hatching fifty offspring at once. But his job is short-lived—once he pushes the babies out into the big, wet world, he's done for that season. And he's not the best dad in the world; after he releases them, he will devour them if they don't swim away fast enough.

Another animal known for primarily male nurturing of the young is the penguin. It takes sixty days for a king penguin to hatch. All the while, the male penguin stands on the ice of Antarctica, keeping the egg warm under his soft feathers.

The male Darwin frog is similarly nurturing. He swallows the eggs of the female and stores them in a sac under his chin. When they hatch, he opens his mouth and the tadpoles swim out.

Then there's the European midwife frog. The male carries the eggs the female has laid wrapped around his legs for three weeks until it's time for them to hatch. Then he heads to the water.

Busy as a (Female) Bee

All worker bees are female, but only the queen has the ability to reproduce. Most worker bees gather nectar to make honey; a few stay behind to guard the queen and her babies.

Just like bees, ants are divided into workers (female) and soldiers (male) who follow a queen, their mother. Worker ants are able to have offspring, but they are not as fertile as the queen. Their role in life is to collect food for the queen and her newborn larvae.

Some unknown someone observed two pythons from India having sex for 180 days.

What mammal has the largest male organs? Scientists tell us it is the right whale, whose penis measures over seven feet and whose testes weigh one ton.

Now why the right whale's penis is larger than that of the blue whale, which is the largest animal on earth, I do not know. Perhaps it has something to do with the fact that female blues are larger than male blues. A full-sized female is about 110 tons.

Blue whales are amazingly large—their hearts weigh 1,000 pounds, their tongues 6,000, and their bones 15,000. Their babies are among the fastest-growing animals in the world. On average, they weigh 4,000 pounds at birth and are fed mother's milk forty times a day, gaining almost 10 pounds per hour. By the age of one, the infant is 50,000 pounds.

All about Elephants

A troop of elephants is always led by females. If males become too aggressive, they are forced to live on their own as rogue elephants. When an elephant dies, the rest of the troop mourns by the body for several days, then covers the corpse in dirt and leaves and moves on. Elephants sometimes visit the graveyards of their deceased kin, touching the dry bones tenderly with their trunks and feet. They are the only mammals, other than humans, that are known to mourn.

These giant beasts also perform mercy killings if a troop member is suffering. After an elephant performs such a task, it washes itself.

Elephants live longer, on average, than any other mammal except humans. The oldest known elephant was a circus elephant named Modoc, who died at the age of seventy-five after surviving a fire in which she rescued the lions by dragging their cage to safety.

Actually elephants never stop growing—the bigger the elephant, the older it is. Their trunks are the longest noses of any animal, and they use them to pick things up and suck water. At the Kenya National Park, they've even learned to turn on water spigots with their trunks.

Elephants are vegetarians, requiring over five hundred pounds of plants each day and forty gallons of water.

They have the longest pregnancies too—twenty-one months. Once the baby is born, Mom has a friend called the auntie elephant who helps with day care.

Know the expression "An elephant never forgets"? Turns out it's true. Folks who train elephants say that it is very hard to teach them something, but once they know it, they have it for life. A scientist proved this once. He taught an elephant to differentiate between two boxes, one marked with a circle and the other a square. It took him over three hundred tries to get it right, but after that, he always knew which one meant food inside. Then the scientist went away, and the elephant was not tested for a year. When he was retested twelve months later, he remembered on the first try.

Stranger than Fiction

In 1547 in France, a mother pig and her six babies were sentenced to death for killing and eating a child. The sow was executed, but the piglets were pardoned because it was felt that they had been led astray by the bad example of their mother.

Flatworms don't worry about the whole male/female thing. When it's time for more worms, they split in two.

The gigantic teeth of hippos are not used to eat food as hippopotami are strict vegetarians. Females use their choppers to defend their babies from crocodiles; males use them to fight one another for the chance to mate with the cutest girls.

Life as a green turtle is tough. A female lays almost two thousand eggs in her life, but only 18 percent hatch and only 3 percent live to breeding age.

Birds Don't Have It So Good Either

Most birds die before they are one, killed by cats, other animals, cars, windows, and disease. In general, the bigger the bird, the longer its life. The oldest known bird is a royal albatross called "Grandma," who's in her late sixties.

A duck's quack doesn't make an echo. No one knows why.

A Story of True Love

Honey guide birds and honey badgers make great bedfellows. They both love honey, but the badger can't find it very well on its own, while the bird, which can find honey just fine, can't break into the hive on its own. So they team up—the bird leads the badger to the tree with its chatter; the badger tears open the hive with its paws and they both feast. No word on what they do about the bee stings.

The swamp antechinus is a tiny Australian marsupial whose males literally die from too much sex. They go into a wild frenzy of intercourse, impregnating as many females as they can until they die of starvation.

Talk about Mother Love

At Bracken Cave in Texas, approximately ten million free-tailed bats are born each year. Each evening, the mothers go out in search of food while the babies cling to the cave walls. Naturalists report that every mother of the ten million comes back to her own offspring. (But how would the rangers know if the bats got the wrong babies, I wonder?)

Virginia Woolf kept a marmoset named Mitz as a pet.

I Want to Be Alone

Jaguars are the Greta Garbos of the cat kingdom. They live alone, only coming together to mate. The female gives birth to two to four kittens and raises them as a single mother. As they reach maturity, they too strike out on their own.

After mating, the male garter snake puts a chastity belt on the female, plugging up her sexual opening with a secretion so that only his genes will be sure to be the ones that are passed on.

Tschingel, a female beagle, was one of the best mountain climbers in the world. In the mid-1800s, she climbed fifty-three peaks of the Alps, eleven of which had never been climbed. When she climbed Mount Blanc in 1875, she was made a member of the Alpine Club. Whether she did this alone or with a human is unclear.

Only female polar bears hibernate—and only when they are pregnant.

Koko, the famous signing gorilla, knew about a thousand words. At age seven, she was given an intelligence test and scored the same as a seven-year-old human.

Sea otters sleep by wrapping themselves up in giant kelp that is attached to the bottom of the ocean; it keeps them anchored in one place.

There are more than 1,900 species of fireflies, and when the male wants to mate with one of his own kind, he flashes a particular signal that the female of his kind responds to.

However, certain females of *other* firefly species have learned to imitate the flash patterns of firefly species that are not their own so they can attract and then eat the hapless boy flies.

Historically, in China they put fireflies inside perforated lanterns to make lights. The glow from only six fireflies is said to provide enough light to read a book.

Cuckoos are lazy mothers. A female cuckoo will wait until other birds are away from their nests, then push one of the eggs out and lay one of her own. The baby cuckoo hatches sooner than the other babies and proceeds to roll all the other eggs out of the nest. The poor foster mother doesn't realize this chick is not her child and nurtures the baby to fledglinghood. Because cuckoos are much larger than the host birds, the poor mother bird figuratively wears her claws to the bone trying to feed the strapping child. Some even lose weight in the process.

Ladybugs get their name from the Virgin Mary, often called Our Lady. They received that exalted name because they are so useful in eating harmful insects in the garden. In England, they are called "ladybirds."

The horses used to deliver mail for the Pony Express were usually female. Calmer, I'd guess.

CHAPTER 6

Women Doing It for Themselves

Just the Facts

Here are some statistics from factmonster.com that give a fascinating glimpse into the way women's lives have changed in the past hundred years or so:

- *No Wonder It's Hard for Some of Us to Get a Date:* There were more men than women in the United States in 1900—100 men for every 95.9 women. By 2002, those figures had essentially reversed; there were only 95.5 men for every 100 women.

- *At the Ivory Towers:* Only twenty-three PhDs were awarded to women in 1900; but by 2018, more women than men earned doctorates in the US; out of nearly 80,000 doctoral degrees that year, 53 percent of the recipients were women. However, women are still significantly underrepresented when it comes to PhDs in STEM fields (Science, Technology, Engineering, and Mathematics).

- *Here's a Truly Astounding Statistic:* The life expectancy for women in 1900 was only 48.3 years; by 1998, it had climbed to almost eighty.

- *We're Tying the Knot Later:* In the early twentieth century, the average age of a woman's first wedding was 21.9; by 2000, it was 25.1, and it has now risen to 27.8.

- *And Untying It More Frequently:* Divorces were exceedingly rare in 1900—only 0.5 percent of the population. By 2006, the divorce rate was 50 percent.

- *Babies Don't Kill Us So Often Anymore:* 6 women out of 100 died in childbirth in 1915; these days, fewer than 0.8 in 1,000 die.

- *At the Office:* 19 percent of women worked outside the home in 1900; by 2000, the figure had skyrocketed to 77 percent.

Now for the Bad News

According to Catalyst, a nonprofit research organization, women made up almost 50 percent of the work force in 2001, but only two Fortune 500 companies had a woman CEO; ninety of the top five hundred corporations had no women officers at all; and of the 410 that did have women officers, only 10 percent had women holding one-quarter or more corporate officer roles.

Sixty-three percent of adults living in poverty are women.

Women account for only 5.4 percent of the top executives at the S & P 500 corporations according to the Pew Research Center.

Women nurses actually make more than male ones—around 5 percent more.

The first woman to fly solo around the world was Ohioan Geraldine Mock. It was 1964—long after a man did it.

In ancient times, the only jobs women could hold in China were as doctors or sorceresses, and until the late nineteenth century, the education of girls was considered a waste of money in most places in the world. In England, for instance, in the seventeenth century, more than 80 percent of all women were illiterate.

We all know that witches were burned at the stake, right? Well, yes, but it turns out that in Salem, the famous witchcraft capital of New England, other methods were preferred. Twenty-five witches died in Salem: Nineteen died by hanging, four died waiting in prison, and one was crushed to death using large stones.

The first woman in Congress was Montana's Jeannette Rankin, who was elected in 1916; Montana had granted women the right to vote three years earlier. Later she ran for Senate but lost because she was a pacifist who spoke out against the United States entering WWI, which was an unpopular position. She was true to her beliefs, though. She was still in the House when the vote was taken to enter WWII. She was opposed to going to war then too.

Meanwhile, the first woman elected to the US Senate was Hattie Caraway in 1932. Her husband had been the senator from Arkansas. When he died, the governor tapped Hattie on the condition that she serve only till the following year's election. Hattie said sure but then enjoyed her new job so much that she ran on her own and won—twice.

Taking Matters into Her Own Hands

In Her Footsteps by Annette Madden is a collection of stories of a hundred heroic black women. Here's one of the women I fell in love with.

Elizabeth Freeman was a slave along with her sisters in the home of Colonel John Ashley in Massachusetts. The Declaration of Independence had been written in 1776 and everyone was talking about freedom, liberty, and equality. Elizabeth listened to these discussions while she served meals. When the Revolutionary War ended in 1781, Elizabeth decided it was time to do something about her own liberty. She left the Ashley household and refused to return. A young lawyer, Theodore Sedgwick, agreed to represent her, arguing that according to the Declaration of Independence and the Massachusetts Constitution adopted in 1780, she should be freed. Her case was heard in 1781 and the jury agreed. The judge even ordered Colonel Ashley to pay Elizabeth thirty shillings in damages. After her victory, she went to work for her lawyer's family. Her court case effectively ended slavery in the state of Massachusetts.

●●●●●●

A potential robbery victim thwarted the man who broke into her house by claiming not to have any cash on hand. "I'd be happy to write you a check," said the very cool cucumber. "Who should I make it out to?" The witless thief wannabe told her his name. She wrote the check and called the cops as soon as he departed, and he was arrested shortly thereafter.

Inventive Young Ladies

Margaret Knight was no fly-by-night inventor. Her creations are still in use today—more than a hundred years later. A child laborer, she was only nine when she went to work in a cotton mill. There she witnessed a steel-tipped shuttle flying off a loom and injuring a coworker. She thought that was not right, so she invented a device that prevented shuttles from coming off the loom. Later she invented a machine that turns out square-bottomed brown paper grocery bags. That device, patented in 1871, is the one manufacturers still use today. Ms. Knight had to fight for her patent, though. A man who had seen her make it claimed it was his idea and used her gender against her in court—how could a woman make such a mechanical device? She proved the idea was hers, though, and went on to be granted twenty-six other patents.

Do you hate cleaning the dirty cat food spoon? I certainly do. But rather than complaining, six-year-old Suzanna Goodin decided to do something about it. She invented a spoon-shaped cat cracker so pets can eat their food and their utensils. That clever idea won Suzanna the grand prize in the Weekly Reader National Invention Contest.

Theresa Thompson was eight and her sister Mary nine when they were granted a patent by the US government in 1960. Their invention? A solar teepee, which they named a Wigwarm.

When she was fourteen, Becky Schroeder had an idea for an invention that is still in use today by doctors and astronauts. Wanting to write in the dark after lights-out time, she took phosphorescent paint and put it under writing paper. When she wrote, the glowing letters shone through. Doctors now use this device to read hospital patients' charts at night without waking them, and astronauts use it when their electrical systems are turned down for recharging.

Chelsea Lannon was a kindergartner helping her mother with her baby brother when she had the thought that a diaper would be more useful if it came with a pocket to hold baby wipes and a tiny powder puff. The patent process being what it is, it was not until she was eight that the patent was actually issued.

Other Ingenious Women

What do bulletproof vests, fire escapes, windshield wipers, and laser printers have in common? They were all invented by women.

In 1914, Mrs. Natalie Stolp was on Philadelphia's mass transit when it occurred to her that abusive men would use the crowds as an excuse to cop a feel and molest female travelers. So she created and patented a device that would attach to a woman's petticoat and jab a sharp needle into anyone who applied pressure to it.

Three French women got the idea in the 1980s to create a diaper that played "When the Saints Go Marching In" when wet.

It was a woman who invented Monopoly. Lizzie Magie had the idea in 1903 and patented it under the name "The Landlord's Game." A man named Charles Darrow later adapted it. At first it was believed to be too complicated to become popular, but proving that pundits don't know all, more than two hundred fifty million games have been sold.

* * * * * *

Four men who were supposed to be on the fatal voyage of the *Titanic* missed the boat because the women in each of their lives had a premonition of danger and begged them not to go. In three cases, it was their wives; in the fourth, his mother-in-law.

Women Warriors

Who says women aren't soldiers? Women have been fighting and taking no prisoners since ancient times, as these excerpts from *Sheroes* by Varla Ventura attest:

- Aba was a warrior who ruled the city of Olbe in the nation of Tencer around 550 BC. She got support from some very high places, such as the likes of Cleopatra VII and Marc Antony! Tencer remained a matriarchy after her rule, with its rulership passing to her female descendants.

- Abra was the queen of Babylon, according to medieval Spanish accounts. Along with Queen Florelle and a flotilla of

50,000 expert women archers, Abra defended her kingdom against the Greeks.

- Ada was the sister of Artemesia, queen of Caria and military advisor to Xeres; and Ada was also a warrior-queen (circa 334 BC) in her own right. The brilliant military strategist Alexander helped her regain her throne from her invasive brother. She led and triumphed in the siege of the capital's acropolis, after which she was able to take the city. Her ferocity was aided by the intense emotions of a cross-gender civil war within her family, "the siege having become a matter of anger and personal enmity," according to Strabo.

- Boudicca was the queen of a tribe in Britain. Her name means "victorious" in the language of the Celts. When the ancient Romans began to occupy Britain, she was having none of it. Her army attacked Roman towns in AD 61 and killed over 70,000 Romans who had settled there. She was reputed to be "tall of person, of a comely appearance, and appareled in a loose gown of many colors. About her neck she wore a chain of gold, and in her hand she bore a spear. She stood a while surveying her army, and being regarded with a reverential silence, she addressed them in an eloquent and impassioned speech." She died in battle at her own hand, taking poison rather than be killed by the enemy.

- At one point the Celtic army had more women than men!

- Cratesipolis was queen of Sicyon around 300 BC. She stood in battle beside her husband, the famous Alexander the Great, and fought on even after he died. She ruled several important Greek cities very successfully and managed a vast army of soldier-mercenaries. She went on to take Corinth for Ptolemy and nearly married him, but the plans fizzled.

- Rhodogune, queen of ancient Parthia in 200 BC, got word of a revolt when she was taking a bath. Vowing to end the uprising before her hair was dressed, she hopped on her horse and rushed to lead her army to defense. True to her word, she directed the entire, lengthy war without ever bathing or combing her hair. Portraits of Rhodogune always faithfully depict her dishevelment. (Another queen of the ancient world, Semiramis, also pulled herself from the bath to the battlefield act when her country needed a brave leader.)

Of the royal lineage of Cleopatra, Zenobia Septimus preferred the hunt to the bath and boudoir. She was queen of Syria for a quarter-century beginning in AD 250 and was quite a scholar, recording the history of her nation. She was famed for her excellence on safari, specializing in the rarified skill of hunting panthers and lions. When the Romans came after Syria, Zenobia disgraced the empire's army in battle, causing them to turn tail and run. This inspired Arabia, Armencia, and Periso to ally with her, and she was named Mistress of Nations. The Romans licked their wounds and enlisted the help of the barbarians they conquered for the Roman army, including Goths, Gauls, Vandals, and Franks, who threatened to march on Zenobia's league of nations. When Caesar Aurelius sent messengers requesting her surrender, she replied, "It is only by arms that the submission you require can be achieved. You forget that Cleopatra preferred death to servitude. When you see me in war, you will repent your insolent proposition." And battle they did. Zenobia fought bravely, holding her city Palmyra against the mass of invaders for longer than anyone thought possible. Upon her capture, Zenobia was taken to Rome in chains, jewels, and her own chariot, and she was given her own villa in Rome, where her daughters went on to intermarry into prominent families who ruled Rome.

Italian Maria Gaetana Agnesi, who lived in the early nineteenth century, was a true child prodigy. By the age of nine, she spoke fluent French, Latin, Greek, and Hebrew in addition to her native Italian and delivered an hour-long speech on the right of women to be educated—in Latin! She was also a mathematical genius who began original work on differential and integral calculus when barely twenty. But her facility in languages didn't go to waste. She used it to bring together mathematicians working in various languages.

The first human cannonball was a woman named Zazel, who was launched into the air through the use of a giant spring inside a cannon.

Legal Eagle

"Charlotte Ray wanted to practice law," writes Annette Madden in *In Her Footsteps*.

But she had a problem—she was a woman and black and it was 1869. But she had the determination she inherited from her father, Charles Ray, editor of the *Colored American* and pastor of Bethesda Congregational Church in New York, who was also known for his work on the Underground Railroad. So, after college and a stint of teaching at Howard University, she began to take law classes and graduated from the Howard University Law School in February 1872. Rules for admission to the bar had been set by the Supreme Court of the District of Columbia. Under those rules, as a graduate of Howard University Law School, she was not required to take a bar examination. Her application went through without a ripple and she was admitted to practice in the lower courts of the District of Columbia in March 1872 and to practice in the Supreme Court of the District of Columbia in April 1872. She promptly opened a law office in Washington, hoping to specialize in real estate law, a field that did not require trial appearances. But she was not able to build up sufficient clientele due to prejudice and the economic depression of the time, and she was forced to give up active practice. However, she still remains the first black woman regularly admitted to the practice of law in any jurisdiction in the United States.

Helping Hands

The YWCA was started in 1855 by Emma Roberts to help single women looking for jobs in London. (Remember, this was a time when single women were not supposed to appear anywhere unaccompanied.) Her mission was to offer safe, inexpensive lodgings, friendship, and moral guidance.

⬤ ⬤ ⬤ ⬤ ⬤ ⬤

Emily Warner was the first female commercial airline pilot in the United States. It was Frontier Airlines that took that bold leap of hiring her in 1973.

The Black Nightingale

We've all heard of Florence Nightingale, but Jamaican Mary Seacole was an equally important figure in the establishment of modern nursing. She was born in the early 1880s in Kingston, Jamaica, to a free black woman and a Scottish Army officer. Her mother taught her two things: Creole medicine and hotelkeeping, skills she put to use as an adult in Jamaica, Colombia, and Panama. When she heard about the Crimean War, she traveled to England to offer her services to the British Army. She was refused because of her color. But Mary was determined, so she made her own way to the Crimea and offered her help to Florence Nightingale herself. Again, the answer was no. So

Mary decided to build her own "hotel for invalids," which was so successful that Mary went deeply into debt caring for the soldiers who flocked there. Like other women before her, she ended up writing her life story. *The Wonderful Adventures of Mrs. Seacole in Many Lands* became a bestseller, and her finances dramatically improved. Ultimately she was honored for her work, winning the Crimean Medal, the French Legion of Honor, and a Turkish medal. But she has never received the kind of historical attention she deserves.

Speaking of famous nurse Florence Nightingale, it turns out she didn't spend a lot of time nursing, only about three years during the Crimean War. Rather, she became famous as an amazing administrator who founded nursing schools.

● ● ● ● ● ●

The wife of Ulysses S. Grant woke one morning in 1865 with the intense sense that she and her husband should get out of Washington, DC, ASAP—that very day, even though it meant standing up President Lincoln's invitation to the theater. That's why Grant was not killed by Booth that evening when the actor assassinated the president. Booth's papers later revealed that Grant was on his hit list.

In 1913, to bring attention to women's right to vote, Emily Davison, a British suffragette, threw herself under a horse owned by the king of England, which was running in the Derby; the experience proved fatal for her.

Julia Child was the very first woman to be given the title of "Chef." The honor, previously given only to men, was bestowed in 1958.

Famous Last Words

Grammarian Dominique Bouhours, who died in 1702, made sure to do it—or rather say it—properly. Her very last words were, "I am about to—or I am going to—die: either expression is used."

Henry VIII was famous for chopping his wives' heads off. One of them, Anne Boleyn, decided to show a little class when it was her turn, declaring the process to be easy because, "The executioner is, I believe, very expert; and my neck is very slender."

On her deathbed, the great ballerina Anna Pavlova, who was known particularly for her dance "Death of the Swan," said, "Get my 'Swan' costume ready!"

The ancient Romans were famous for killing themselves if dishonored. And if the emperor commanded you to kill yourself, you were supposed to pick up the knife and do it unflinchingly. Caecine Paetus didn't relish the idea when it was his turn. His wife Arria, however, was made of sterner stuff. Holding up the knife, she jammed it into her breast, proclaiming, "Paetus, it doesn't hurt!"

⊛ ⊛ ⊛ ⊛ ⊛ ⊛

Clare Boothe Luce led a fascinating life. One story that gets told about her often is how she tried to convert the pope. It was when Luce was the US ambassador to Italy. She had recently converted to Catholicism and was granted a private audience with the Pope Pius XII. The audience went on for hours, which was very atypical. Finally, writes Nino Lo Bello in *The Incredible Book of Vatican Facts and Papal Curiosities*, Vatican aides "peeked into the room and saw the pope backed into a corner with Mrs. Luce talking a blue streak. Finally getting a word in edgewise, Pius XII was heard to say, 'But, Mrs. Luce, I already am a Roman Catholic!' "

Mary Manley, political journalist and author, was the first woman to be jailed for her writing. The book? Her tongue-twisting satire *Secret Memoirs and Manners of Several Persons of Quality of Both Sexes from the New Atlantis, an Island in the Mediterranean* was a challenge to the Tory opposition, the Whigs. But the old adage about any kind of publicity—even bad publicity—being good held true: the book was an instant bestseller.

Women's Hall of Shame

In 1939, world-renowned singer Marian Anderson was banned from singing in Washington's Constitutional Hall because of her color.

Noah's wife had no name—at least none that we know. She is only referred to in the Bible as "Noah's Wife."

The only women to appear on US currency are Pocahontas, Sacajawea, Susan B. Anthony, and Martha Washington, who was also the only woman featured on a US currency note. Her likeness appeared on the face of the one dollar Silver Certificate of 1886 and 1891 and the back of the one dollar Silver Certificate of 1896.

In 1893, New Zealand became the first country in the world to give women the vote (though they couldn't hold office until later). It wasn't until 1920 that women in the United States had that right. Several women ran for election in Finland in 1907, the first year the country had elections. Some even won, making Finland the first parliament to include women.

The First Ten Women in Space

1. Valentina Tereshkova, 1963 (USSR)

2. Svetlana Savitskaya, 1982 (USSR)

3. Sally Ride, 1983 (USA)

4. Judith Resnick, 1984 (USA)

5. Kathryn Sullivan, 1984 (USA)

6. Anna Fisher, 1984 (USA)

7. Margaret Seddon, 1985 (USA)

8. Shannon Lucid, 1985 (USA)

9. Loren Acton, 1985 (USA)

10. Bonnie Dunbar, 1985 (USA)

In ancient Egypt, between 3500 and circa 2500 BC, the only career not open to women was judge.

Women have been keeping their own names after marriage for centuries in Iceland.

The first three elected women heads of modern countries were:

1. Sirimavo Bandaranaike, Sri Lanka, 1960–1965 and 1970–1977

2. Indira Gandhi, India, 1966–1977 and 1980–1984

3. Golda Meir, Israel, 1969–1974

The very first person to go over Niagara Falls and live was Annie Edison Taylor, who did it in 1901 in a wooden barrel. It would be ten years before a man replicated her feat—and he used a steel barrel.

Tragic Oversight

The unsung mothers of computer programming are six women named Jean Bartik, Netty Holberton, Marlyn Meltzer, Ruth Teitelbaum, Kay Antonelli, and Frances Spence who met during war work in 1945. Their job, along with many other women, was to calculate bullet trajectories for American artillery gunmen. Only women did this work, for the army believed that only the fairer sex had the patience to do something so boring. They called such women "computers." Then, one day, the six women were sent to work with ENIAC, the first electronic computer, which had been designed to do by machine the calculations these women had been doing. The six, completely on their own, were assigned the task of programming this gargantuan machine, a job the military considered a clerical function. They literally created the field of programming without a shred of credit from the powers that be. They were not even invited to a gala dinner celebrating the first successful test run of their program nor the fiftieth anniversary celebration of the computer in 1995.

A Measure of How Far We've Come?

In 2000, Barbie took on a new role—running for president. Candidate Barbie was dressed for the race in a blue suit complete with a "Barbie for President" button. Proving presidents can be glamorous, she also came with a red gown and heels. Presidential Barbie was packaged with a copy of the White House Project's Girls' Action Agenda, which urged girls to pursue leadership roles.

According to the US Department of Labor, the ten occupations with the highest median weekly earnings among women who were full-time wage and salary workers in 2006 were:

1. Pharmacists, $1,564

2. Chief executives, $1,422

3. Lawyers, $1,333

4. Physicians and surgeons, $1,329

5. Computer and information systems managers, $1,300

6. Computer software engineers, $1,272

7. Physical therapists, $1,086

8. Management analysts, $1069

9. Medical and health services managers, $1,064

10. Computer scientist and systems analysts, $1,039

CHAPTER 7

Saintly Manifestations and Royal Subjects

Queen Christina of Sweden, who ruled in the 1600s, had a tiny problem—she was absolutely terrified of fleas. So afraid, in fact, that she commissioned the construction of a tiny cannon for her bedroom, which she used to fire itty-bitty cannonballs at the pesky critters. No word on how successful a shot she was, but apparently it was an activity on which she spent hours per day.

Of the top eight richest royals in the world, only one is a woman—Queen Beatrix of the Netherlands, who is reputed to be worth around $4.7 billion.

The largest private art collection in the world—with more than 250,000 works—is owned by England's Queen Elizabeth.

Sigrid Storrade was queen of Denmark when the king of Norway, Harold Graenska, asked her to marry him. Apparently his request displeased her, for she had him assassinated instead.

The capital of Ethiopia was founded by a woman; Taitu was the fourth wife of Menelik II, who was emperor of Ethiopia from 1889 to 1913. Using wifely persuasion, she talked him into building a home near a warm spring and donating the land around it to the nobility. She named it Addis Ababa, which means "new flower."

Contrary to legend, Queen Isabella did not hock her jewelry to pay for Christopher Columbus's voyage to the New World. She just used it as a threat to force her husband, King Ferdinand, to cough up the dough.

Rumor has it that Mary, Queen of Scots (who reigned from 1688 to 1694) and Anne of Great Britain (whose reign was from 1702 to 1714) were both lesbians. Mary also has the distinction of being one of the youngest rulers of all times—she was only one week old when she was crowned queen but was sent to France as an infant to protect her from the Scottish infighting going on at the time. There she was wed as a teenager to the future king of France, who died shortly thereafter, leaving her a (virgin?—there are rumors that the marriage was never consummated) widow at eighteen.

Queen Mary I of England and Ireland was a Catholic who had Protestants tortured and killed. Her actions provoked the nickname "Bloody Mary," which inspired the cocktail.

Napoleon's wife Josephine used so much perfume (musk was her scent) that those waiting on her would faint from the smell.

When Josephine married Napoleon, he had a surprise when he came to the nuptial bed—his new wife insisted that he learn to sleep with her dog, Fortune. Sleeping wasn't the problem. That first night, when he was making love to his bride, Fortune, believing Josephine was being harmed, bit the future emperor on the leg, leaving a permanent scar.

Catherine the Great once saw a primrose in her garden and fell in love with it, setting a guard over it to protect it from harm.

Spain's Queen Isabella was the first woman to appear on a US postage stamp.

Isabeau, who was queen of France in the late twelfth century, was renowned for her beauty. To keep her looks, she used a beauty regimen that included bathing in asses' milk and rubbing crocodile glands and the brains of boars on her skin. She was the first one during the Middle Ages to bare her bosom in low-cut gowns; the fad quickly spread.

Queen Wilhelmina of the Netherlands (who reigned from 1890 to 1948) and Queen Victoria of Great Britain (who reigned from 1837 to 1901) hold the distinction of being two of the longest-reigning monarchs in history.

"I am said to be the most beautiful woman in Europe. About that, of course, I cannot judge because I cannot know. But about the other queens, I know. I am the most beautiful queen in Europe."

—Marie, Queen of Romania

Hail Victoria!

Victoria was used to having her way. Once when she was mad at the Bolivians, she commanded her navy to go and sink their fleet. But they are a landlocked country, explained her admirals, so they do not have a fleet. Hearing the news, she snatched up a pair of scissors and a map and cut the offending country out of the world.

In 1996, Sotheby's, the famous auction house, auctioned off a pair of Queen Victoria's underpants.

When Queen Victoria wed Prince Albert, their wedding cake weighed three hundred pounds, and at the top was a foot-high statute of Britannica blessing the couple, who were dressed in Roman togas.

Speaking of royal wedding customs, when French royals wed, it used to be the practice to release two hundred dozen birds into the air as the royal party crossed to the Palais. That's 2,400 winged creatures all soaring at once, for those who want the exact count.

Incredible Cleo

Cleopatra was one amazing dame. I found all 1,131 pages of her fictionalized autobiography written by Margaret George quite compelling. Here's some of the best dish from there and other sources:

- The most famous queen of the Nile was not Egyptian. She was Macedonian, a descendent of the sister of Alexander the Great, who conquered Egypt. She was the only ruler in her line who actually learned to speak Egyptian.

- In order to keep the Egyptian royal blood pure, her line, the Ptolemys, practiced marriage only between siblings and were considered gods and goddesses, just like the Pharaohs. She at first resisted the tradition because she believed it promoted terrible sibling rivalry but eventually gave in.

- She was said to be under five feet, extremely voluptuous, with a big nose. Whether she was beautiful is the focus of much academic argument.

- Her official titles were the Seventh Cleopatra of the Royal House of Ptolemy; the Queen; the Lady of the Two Lands; Thea Philopator, the Goddess Who Loves Her Father; Thea Neotera, the Younger Goddess; the daughter of Ptolemy; Neos Dionysus, the New Dionysus.

- Married to both Julius Caesar and Marc Antony as well as her two brothers, she had four children. The oldest, by Caesar, was killed by Caesar's nephew Octavian, who feared his cousin taking the thrones of Rome and Egypt. Her three remaining children, all by Antony, were raised in Rome by Octavian, and one briefly served as king of Egypt until he was murdered by Caligula.

- She was a worshiper of the goddess Isis.

- Ascending to the throne at age eighteen, she was a very effective ruler; her reign brought unparalleled prosperity and peace throughout Egypt, which was then the richest country in the world. She stored grain for famine; she had the Nile dredged to prevent overflooding.

- After warring with her siblings, she really did sneak back into her palace in Alexandria rolled into a carpet to meet Julius Caesar.

- To meet Antony, she really did do herself up as Venus and sail to him, but not in a barge, which was not seaworthy. And she did give a dinner for him that employed millions of rose petals to create a carpet that was a foot deep.

- She did swallow the largest pearl in the world, which she pretended to dissolve in a glass of wine to win a bet with Antony, but retrieved it later. It was far too valuable to flush down the toilet, so to speak.

- She probably killed herself with a cobra, not an asp, after her empire fell to Octavian and Marc Antony died, in order to avoid being taken to Rome and displayed as a conquered monarch.

There is a French plum called *reine-claude*. It's so named because it reminded folks of the bottom of the wife of François I, Queen Claude, who was quite round.

When something is "Florentine," it is made with spinach. But do you know why? It's because Catherine de' Medici, who was from Florence and went to France to marry the king, loved spinach. In fact, she insisted that the green vegetable be served every meal of her life.

Spanish Queen Juana so loved her husband, Philip, that when he passed away in 1506, she carried his coffin with her for the rest of her life, refusing to allow him to be buried.

Time magazine named Wallis Simpson, the duchess of Windsor, Person of the Year in 1936 because the king of England had given up his throne for her. "In the entire history of Great Britain," wrote *Time*, "there has been only one voluntary royal abdication, and it came about in 1936 solely because of one woman, Mrs. Simpson."

Ever Prepared

The British royals always travel with mourning clothes so that they will be properly attired should someone important die.

That fact was revealed in 1952 when Elizabeth, still a princess at the time, was on a trip in Africa with Philip. Notified that her father had died and she was now queen, Elizabeth instantly appeared in appropriate outfits.

In a tradition started during the reigns of King George V and King George VI, the royal incumbent gives out Christmas pudding to her staff each holiday season. Elizabeth II has given out 78,000 puddings since she became queen.

Poor Princess Caroline of Brunswick. Her wedding to the future British King George IV was an unmitigated disaster. Her groom was so inebriated before the ceremony that he had to be carried down the aisle, and he tried to get up and leave before it was over. (His father forced him bodily to sit down again.) When asked if anyone knew any reason why the marriage shouldn't take place, he burst into tears.

The Queen of Sheba

Many people consider the origins of the queen of Sheba an unsolvable mystery. Not so in Ethiopia, writes Annette Madden in *In Her Footsteps*.

> It is certain that the woman who entranced King Solomon was the Ethiopian queen named Makeda. According to the Kebra Nagast ("Glory of the Kings"), a revered Ethiopian history, Queen Makeda was born in 1020 BC. Upon her father's death, the beautiful and wealthy Makeda ascended the throne.
>
> An Ethiopian merchant prince named Tamrin engaged in trade with King Solomon of Jerusalem and was impressed with the king's honest and impartial nature. He shared his opinion with Makeda, who was impressed with the de-

scription of this just—and rich—man, and she determined to travel to Jerusalem to meet him. Tamrin put together a caravan and guided Makeda's entourage on the journey.

In Jerusalem, Makeda was welcomed by Solomon in royal fashion. He supplied her and her entourage with housing in his palace and wined and dined them, paying special attention to the beauteous Makeda. The two royal personages were delighted with each other's company. Solomon even converted her to his religion, Judaism.

After six months, Makeda informed Solomon that as much as she would love to stay, she had to return to her duties in Sheba. Solomon was reluctant to let her leave and pleaded with her to remain a short while longer. Makeda agreed. During this continued stay, she became pregnant with Solomon's child. Finally, she insisted that she must return to her country, and reluctantly Solomon saw her on her way, giving her many presents and a ring for the unborn child he hoped would be a son. Shortly after she returned to Sheba, she did indeed give birth to a son, naming him Ebna Hakim, which means "son of the wise man."

According to the legend, when their son was twenty-two, she sent him to visit his father, as she had promised when she left Jerusalem. Solomon reportedly was overjoyed to see his son, especially since his other heir, Rheabom, was reported to be somewhat foolish. Solomon pleaded with Ebna Hakim to stay in Jerusalem and become his successor, but Ebna insisted on returning to Sheba, and Solomon reluctantly let him go, sending with him the sons of his counselors, trained in Hebrew law, to help with the conversion of the people of Sheba to Judaism. Reportedly, these young men stole the Ark of the Covenant from Jerusalem and took it with them to what is now Ethiopia, where the Ethiopians claim it still remains. The missionaries were successful in their work, forming a community of the Falasha (Black Jews), who still form a significant part of the Ethiopian population.

England's Queen Eleanor was a loving wife. When her husband Edward I was felled by a poisoned arrow, she personally sucked the poison out, saving the king. Unfortunately, she died.

As the future ruler of England, Queen Elizabeth II was determined to help with the war effort during World War II. But there was to be no wimpy bandage rolling for her. At eighteen, she enrolled in a class in heavy mechanics, learning to strip and service engines. She took to it so well that even after the war she did it as a hobby.

Margaret, the "Maid of Norway," was named queen of Scotland when she was only three years old. But it wasn't until she was seven, in 1290, that she set forth on a ship to claim her throne. She never made it, dying of seasickness on the way.

Lady Jane Grey was only queen for nine days before she was executed at the age of sixteen.

The Queen Who Was King

Nzinga, the daughter of the king of the Ndongo people (in the land now known as Angola), was born in the late 1500s. Her people were at war with the Portuguese, who were trying to enslave them. Trained by her father, she supposedly killed her first enemy at twelve years old. Eventually her father was overthrown, and her brother took the throne as the fighting with the Portuguese continued. "When the situation reached a stalemate," reports *In Her Footsteps*, "the Portuguese governor requested a ceasefire. Nzinga was sent to negotiate."

Nzinga arrived with all the pomp and circumstance of a royal procession, preceded by musicians and accompanied by several handmaidens. There was only one chair in the room of the meeting, the governor's throne. Instead of sitting on the pillows that were offered to her, which would have denoted her lesser status, she reportedly summoned one of her women servants, had her kneel on her hands and knees and then used her as a chair.

Her keen intelligence and her immense dignity impressed the Portuguese. One of the methods she used to gain their confidence during the extended negotiations was to accept their religion. She was baptized into the Catholic faith in the cathedral of Luanda, taking the name Dona Ana de Souza, with the governor and his wife acting as godparents.

Finally, with Nzinga's help, a peaceful agreement was settled on. However, the Portuguese did not stick to the terms of the agreement. War broke out again, Nzinga's brother was defeated, and in 1623, at the age of forty-one, she became absolute ruler of her country. She and her people were forced east by the Portuguese, where she established the kingdom of Matamba. When dissension arose among her subjects about her rule, she quickly moved to consolidate her power, changing the law so that she was no longer called Queen, but King. She even had a harem of young men as her "wives." After this she sometimes wore men's clothing, usually when leading her troops in battle, proving that clothes not only make the man, but the woman as well.

She never ceased to oppose Portuguese rule, although in 1659 she signed a treaty with the Portuguese in the face of their superior weaponry. She was then seventy-five and had been fighting the Portuguese most of her adult life. She died on December 17, 1663, after which the Portuguese were able to rapidly expand their slave trade in the region.

The queen of England has an annual budget of $20.3 million, paid for by the British people. This includes her salary—about eight million a year; the rest is for living expenses, although upkeep on all the palaces and the royal yacht comes out of other national expense accounts.

Life Was Tough, Even for Royalty

Queen Anne of England, who lived in the late seventeenth century, gave birth to seventeen children, but only one made it past infancy. And that one died at age twelve.

Being a royal has its perks. It's no wonder these lovely ladies tried to impersonate them. However, in each case, the hoax was discovered:

- Anna Anderson claimed to be Anastasia, the daughter of the last Russian Czar Nicholas II.

- Stella Chaippini tried to convince folks she was the queen of France.

- Sarah Wilson was a royal maid who was caught stealing from England's Queen Charlotte, wife of George III, and was banished from Britain in 1771. Sent to the United States, she decided to try to pretend she was Princess Susanna Caroline Matilda, Queen Charlotte's sister. She was appropriately wined and dined throughout the colonies until the truth finally got out.

The Comtesse de Noailles, who lived during the nineteenth century, was a tad eccentric. Wherever she went, she insisted that a herd of cows be pastured under her bedroom window, believing that the methane gas they gave off in the process of digestion was good for her. She also was known for sleeping with the hide of a Norwegian wildcat on top of her and a pair of socks that were stuffed with squirrel fur wrapped around her head.

In the sixteenth century, Lady Glamis was accused of witchcraft and trying to murder the king of Scotland and was burned at the stake. She now haunts Glamis Castle in Angus, Scotland. Many visitors have seen her floating above the clock tower. Meanwhile, Anne Boleyn, Catherine Howard, and Jane Seymour are all said to haunt Hampton Court Palace in London.

The Right Stuff

Marie Antoinette, on her way to the guillotine, is reported to have said in response to some remark to be brave, "Courage! I have shown it for years; you think I shall lose it at the moment when my sufferings are to end?"

The Lowdown on the Firsts

We don't have queens in the United States. The closest we come, aside from movie and pop stars, are the presidents' wives. Here's some good gossip:

- Lady Bird Johnson loved *Gunsmoke* so much that even if she were in the middle of an official function, she would slip out to tune in.

- William McKinley's wife was prone to seizures. No problem, said the prez. Anytime she had a fit in public, he would throw a handkerchief over her head until it was over. She is now believed to have suffered from epilepsy.

"One man can make a difference and every man should try."

—Jacqueline Kennedy Onassis

- The only first lady born outside the United States was John Quincy Adams's wife, Louisa. Born in London, she had an American father and a British mother.

- For fun, Louisa Adams raised silkworms in the White House mulberry trees and spun their silk.

- George Washington wrote most of Martha's correspondence for her because she was functionally illiterate. (But remember, this was in the days before women were widely educated.)

- James Monroe's wife, Elizabeth, requested that the help call her "Your Majesty."

- Mrs. Theodore Roosevelt hated shaking hands. But being a politician's wife, she was called upon to do so a great deal. So she strategized a solution—in a receiving line, she would always hold a bouquet of flowers and bow instead.

- Although John Kennedy was the youngest president, Jackie Kennedy was not the youngest first lady. She was thirty-one when her husband took office. But Frances Cleveland, wife of Grover, was only twenty-one, and Julia Taylor (wife of Zachary) was twenty-four. Both were wed to men more than twice their ages.

- Speaking of Julia Taylor, she so avoided public life that many Washington insiders didn't even know the president had a wife until 1850, when she attended his funeral after he died in office.

- Calvin Coolidge's wife, Grace, loved baseball. in fact, she was dubbed by the media "the number one Boston Red Sox fan."

- Edith Wilson claimed to be a descendent of Pocahontas.

- Fed up with the constant paparazzi, Jacqueline Kennedy Onassis purportedly administered a professional judo flip to a New York news photographer for taking pictures of her outside a movie house in 1969.

- Lucy Hayes, wife of Rutherford B. Hayes, was the first First Lady ever to obtain a college degree.

- Harry and Bess Truman met when they were five. It was love at first sight, he later claimed, because she was the only girl in Independence, Missouri, who could whistle through her teeth.

- The only child born in the White House was Esther Cleveland in 1893, the daughter of Grover and Frances Cleveland.

- Mary Todd Lincoln was not an easy woman to be married to. She was a compulsive shopper who once bought a handkerchief for $80 and a $4,000 bolt of fabric (remember, this was Civil War–era money). Once, in a particularly profligate time, she purchased three hundred pairs of gloves in four months.

- Eleanor Roosevelt was the wife of President Franklin D. Roosevelt and a powerful force to be reckoned with in her own right. What many people don't realize is that she was a niece of President Teddy Roosevelt's and a distant cousin of her husband's. As a result, she didn't have to change her name when she married because she was already Eleanor Roosevelt.

Scintillating Saints

The early Christian saints really got tortured, either by others or through self-inflicted wounds of one sort or another. Whatever the reasons, these women's lives and deaths tended to the extreme:

- Apollinia is the patron saint of toothache sufferers. That's because the Romans tortured her by pulling out all her teeth in an attempt to get her to forsake Christianity. She didn't and saved the Romans the task of burning her at the stake by jumping into the fire of her own accord. Her teeth and jaws are on display at churches throughout Europe.

- Agatha is the patron saint of nurses and those suffering from breast disease, among others. That's because when she thwarted the intentions of a Roman senator, he cut off her breasts. Because she was so holy, Saint Peter restored them. Then she was burned at the stake, which didn't work either because an earthquake interrupted the proceedings. Finally, the Romans cut off her head. She is usually pictured in paintings with her breasts on a plate.

- Brigid, the patron saint of milkmaids, fugitives, newborns, and nuns, among others, was a milkmaid who throughout her life was able to increase the amount of butter in a household. Very pious, the extraordinarily beautiful Irish maiden took a vow of chastity but was having trouble with it because so many men coveted her. So she prayed to be deformed, and amazingly, one of her eyes grew so large that she looked hideous and the other virtually disappeared. Convinced that she would not be able to attract a suitor, her father let her enter the convent, where she continued to make butter multiply and turn her bath water into beer if visiting priests needed it.

- Catherine of Alexandria was a beautiful Egyptian queen who converted many people to Christianity before she was killed by the Roman emperor. Killing her proved difficult, though. He had her spread out on a wheel to be pulled apart, but before she could be hurt, angels appeared...and struck it with lightning and destroyed it. Then they chopped off her head, but instead of blood, milk flowed out as she died. She is the saint unmarried women pray to for a wealthy and handsome husband.

- The patron saint of psychiatrists is Christina the Astonishing, who flew out of her coffin during her funeral mass, roosting in the rafters of the church. Apparently, she had been in a catatonic state and not dead. She said she came back from the dead to help the suffering souls in purgatory be released. She spent the rest of her life on top of towers, perching on weathervanes and other high places to avoid smells (she found the odor of men particularly offensive).

Gemma Galgani, the patron saint of hospital pharmacists, was the sickly daughter of a pharmacist who lived in Italy in the early twentieth century. After praying one day, she received the stigmata (the marks that Christ had from being hung on the cross) and gushed blood from her hands, feet, and sides constantly. At twenty-five, she died with her arms outstretched as if on a cross.

Gwen is the patron saint of nursing mothers, and she is particularly suited to the task, having received the gift of a third breast when she gave birth to triplets. As far as we know, she died a natural death.

Imelda was an Italian saint who created altars in her crib. Very young, she begged to receive her First Communion, saying, "How can anyone receive Jesus into his heart and not die?" Not yet, said religious authorities. Then, one day, a Host flew out of the priest's hand and floated over her head, so he gave it to her. And yes, she did die immediately. She is now the patron saint of first communicants.

When Lucy's mother was cured of an ailment through a visit to a shrine, the young Sicilian pledged herself to perpetual chastity. This didn't make her fiancé happy, who told the Roman authorities on her. She was sentenced to a whorehouse but literally couldn't be budged from the spot, so they decided to burn her at the stake. That didn't work either. Because her fiancé had always admired her eyes, she plucked them out and gave them to him before finally being killed with a sword. She is now the patron saint of those suffering eye disease, among other ailments, and she is the one that Venetian gondoliers sing of when they croon "Santa Lucia." She is their patron as well.

- Another saint with eye-plucking tendencies was Triduana, who took out the offending orbs and had them sent on a dish to the Scottish chief who had fallen in love with her. She is said to protect against eye disease.

- Margaret, a virgin who vowed to stay that way, was thrown into prison by a disgruntled would-be husband. While she was incarcerated, Satan appeared to her in the form of a dragon who ate her, but she was saved when a cross she carried grew so large it split the dragon in two and she escaped unscathed. Eventually she did die when the authorities chopped off her head. Joan of Arc claimed to hear Margaret's voice, among others, counseling her as she went about her deeds. Because of the dragon incident, she is known as the patron saint of childbirth.

- Pearl was a glamorous entertainer in Antioch who, once she became converted to Christianity, moved to Jerusalem and lived as a male hermit known as Pelagius, the "beardless monk." She is now known as Pelagia, the patron saint of actresses.

- Rita was a fourteenth-century woman married to an Italian gangster who beat her. When he was murdered after eighteen years of such abuse, she prayed that her two sons would not try to avenge his death. Rita's prayers were answered; instead, her sons died of some mysterious illness. Unencumbered by family, she decided to become a nun. But the convent would not have her until one day when she appeared inside their locked quarters. Asking Jesus to share his suffering on the cross, a thorn from his statue flew out and stabbed her in her head, where a wound festered for the rest of her life. The odor of her wound changed to roses upon her death and can still be smelled in the convent over six hundred years later. You can also see her body there in a glass case, for it has never decayed.

- Uncumber was the Christian daughter of the pagan king of Portugal, who sought to marry her off. Like so many other female saints, she had taken a vow of chastity and was therefore unwilling to wed. So one night she prayed to become ugly and woke up with a mustache and full beard. In retaliation, her father had her crucified. Dying, she promised to help women escape from unwanted advances from men, hence her name.

The Also-Rans

Christina, Clementina, and Matilda are the only three laywomen to be interred in St. Peter's Basilica. They were granted this honor because of their unusual devotion to the Catholic Church.

- Christina was the Protestant queen of Sweden who abdicated her throne to become a Catholic in 1654 and moved to Rome. She was a huge celebrity as well as a collector of books and artwork and was the patroness of composers.

- From a very wealthy family, Clementina Maria Sobieski married James III of England, but not without misadventure. She was kidnapped on her way to him by the Austrian emperor, escaping over the Alps by herself. Her marriage produced two sons, one of who became an Italian cardinal.

- The first woman buried in St. Peter's was Countess Matilda Canossa. Born in 1046, Matilda was Italy's Joan of Arc, having inherited the rule of northern Italy at the age of nine. She first came to the attention of the church at eighteen when she led a cavalry force against an antipope. Her lover at the time was a monk called Hildebrand of Sovana, who went on to become Pope Gregory VII. But Gregory's papal seat was soon under fire from the German emperor, and Matilda took up her sword again. Though she never won a battle, in time the German emperor got tired of fighting her and gave up.

Stories still circulate that the Catholic Church once had a woman pope—John VIII. According to the story, he was really Joan, not John, whose identity was discovered when she gave birth while riding a horse in a religious procession. The outraged faithful dragged the duplicitous pope through the streets and stoned her to death but kept the baby, who grew up to be a bishop, alive. The Catholic Church denies such an occurrence.

Bible Babes

According to Talmudic tradition, Lilith was Adam's first wife, who left him after a fight. God punished her for disobeying him with the death of a hundred of her demon children every day. Now she avenges herself by harming children and seducing men. Scholars say the biblical figure is derived from a winged Sumerian goddess, also called Lilith.

Eve's name comes from a word that means "life," and her title is "mother of all living." She died six days after Adam, after begging God not to let her live without him.

Hagar was an Egyptian concubine given to Abraham by Sarah when she could not conceive. Hagar gave birth to Ishmael, and eventually Sarah bore Isaac. Each child's descendants formed a line—Isaac's gave rise to the Israelites and Ishmael's the Bedouins.

Rebekah was the wife of Isaac, who found her at a well and married her. (This was apparently a not so uncommon pickup spot, as you will see.) Like Isaac's mother, she had a great deal of trouble getting pregnant, but eventually she succeeded and bore the twins Esau and Jacob, who are said to have hated each other so fiercely that they tried to kill each other in her womb.

When he was grown, Jacob fell in love with Rachel, whom he met at a well, and entered her father's household to work for seven years to make the money to pay her bride price. Finally the wedding day arrived, but her father substituted her older sister Leah, behind a veil. Jacob didn't realize the switch until it was too late. Because he couldn't get out of the marriage and couldn't live without Rachel, he married her a week later and worked another seven years to pay for her. Leah quickly bore Jacob four sons, but Rachel had trouble conceiving. To maintain her wifely status, she offered Jacob a surrogate mother, with whom he had two sons that Rachel raised as hers. She eventually gave birth on her own but died in childbirth delivering her second son. She and Leah are considered the matriarchs of Israel.

Deborah, the "mother of Israel," lived around 1125 BC. She was a prophet, the only woman judge in the Hebrew Bible, and a great warrior who was crucial in securing land in Palestine for the Jews. The resulting poem about her life, "The Song of Deborah" is one of the oldest known pieces of biblical literature. Her last words were, "The dead cannot help the living." After her death, there was peace for seven years.

Abigail is said to have been one of the four most beautiful women in Old Testament history, the others being Sarah, wife of Abraham; Rahab; and Esther, who saved the Jews from Persian slaughter. Abigail means "the father's joy." She is renowned for saving her husband Nabal by intervening with the great King David. When her husband died soon thereafter of natural causes, she wedded David and bore him at least one child.

Great Goddesses!

Incarnations of the divine in feminine form have been worshiped throughout the world. Here is a by no means complete list:

CELTIC

- Danu was the mother of the Tuatha De Danaan, the most important race of people in Celtic mythology.

- Brigid gave the Irish their language.

- Cerridwen brought intelligence and learning to humans.

- Caillech, the daughter of the moon, was the wisest woman. She could move mountains.

CHINESE

- Kuan Yin is the goddess of compassion, often symbolized with a thousand arms representing her vast desire and ability to help. She also represents wisdom and purity.

- The Chinese goddess Ma-Ku personifies the goodness in all people. She took land from the sea and planted it with mulberry trees. She freed the slaves from her cruel father.

EGYPTIAN

- Nut existed before time, before creation. She is the goddess of the heavens. The stars are speckles on her divine body.

- Isis is the goddess of law, healing, and fertility. The wife of Osiris, the god of the underworld, she is the one who brought agriculture to the world.

- Hathor is the protector of all things feminine, including cows.

- Tefnut is the goddess of the dew, very important in a desert land.

- Bastet is the cat goddess, and her temples are full of cats.

- Neith is the Mother goddess.

- Sekhmet is the goddess with a lion's head.

GREEK AND ROMAN

- Aphrodite is the Greek goddess who brought love and beauty into the world and kept them alive. The word aphrodisiac comes from her name. Her Roman name is Venus. Venus possessed a magical mirror; whoever looked into the glass saw only beauty reflected back. When Venus misplaced the treasure, a shepherd found it. He was so taken by his new and improved reflection that he refused to return it. Venus dispatched her son, Cupid, to retrieve it. The two struggled and the mirror shattered. Everywhere a sliver fell, a flower grew.

- The Greek goddess Artemis rules over the hunt and over women in childbirth. Her Roman name is Diana.

- Athena is the Greek goddess of crafts, war, and wisdom. Her Roman name is Minerva.

- Demeter is the Greek goddess who makes all things grow. Her Roman name is Ceres, from which we get the word *cereal*.

- Gaea is the Greek goddess of the Earth. Her Roman name is Terra.

- Hera, wife of Zeus, is the Greek protector of women and the institution of marriage. Her Roman name is Juno.

- Hestia is the Greek goddess of the hearth and home. Her Roman name is Vesta.

- Eos is the Greek goddess of the dawn. It was thought that she emerged every day from the ocean and rose into the sky on a chariot drawn by horses. The morning dew represents her tears of grief for her slain son.

- Hygieia is the Greek goddess of health. The daughter of Aesculapius, the god of medicine and healing, she is responsible for maintaining the atmosphere and is capable of warding off pestilence. The word hygiene is derived from her name.

- A Greek goddess of retribution, Nemesis is responsible for the equilibrium of the universe, granting rewards and issuing punishments when appropriate.

HAWAIIAN

- Pele is the powerful Hawaiian goddess of fire, who lives in the Kilauea Volcano and rules over the family of fire gods.

- Hiiaka is the youngest sister of Pele. She is a fierce warrior and yet a kind and calm friend of humanity. She gave people the healing arts, the creative arts, and the gift of storytelling.

INDIAN

- Durga is the omnipotent goddess of war.

- The goddess of destruction is Kali.

- Lakshmi is the goddess of fortune and wealth and is most usually considered the queen goddess, for she is the wife of Vishnu.

- Sarasvati rules wisdom and learning, in particular the arts and music.

- Parvati is the wife of Shiva.

NATIVE AMERICAN

- Sedna is the goddess of sea creatures. The Inuit people believed that anyone who dared to look at her would be struck dead.

- Selu is the Corn Mother of the Cherokee who cut open her breast so that corn could spring forth and give life to the people.

- Blue Corn Woman and White Corn Maiden are the first mothers of the Tewa people. Blue is the summer mother; White is the winter.

- The Three Sisters are the life-giving forces of corn, beans, and squash of the Iroquois.

- White-Painted Mother is the mother of Child of the Water, from whom all Apaches are descended in spiritual tradition. She keeps her child safe in her womb, slays all evil monsters, and keeps the world safe for Apaches.

- White Buffalo Calf Woman is the giver of the sacred Pipe, which represents truth, for the Lakota.

- Salt Mother is revered by the Hopi, who believe that the Warrior Twins hid salt away from people as a punishment.

NORSE

- Freyja is the goddess of fertility, love, and beauty. Frigg is also a goddess of fertility and creativity.

- Idun is the goddess who brings spring each year.

- Skadi is the goddess of the mountains.

- The Norns are three sisters who live around the tree of life. They control the past, present, and future.

Other Goddess-Inspired Words

- *Money:* From Juno Monets, the Roman goddess of money.

- *Panacea:* Also the name of the Roman goddess who cures illness.

- *Iridescent:* For Iris, the Greek goddess of the rainbow.

- *Peony:* Flowers named for the Greek goddess Paeonia.

Mythological Mamas

Mythology is full of vengeful women and other female creatures:

- The Maenads were fierce creatures. They included Agave, who shredded her son, Pentheus, to pieces, thinking he was a lion. She then paraded around proudly holding his decapitated head up for all to see. Her husband met a similar end.

- Agave, *Sheroes* informs us, "was a Moon-Goddess and was in charge of some of the revelries that were the precedent for Dionysus' cult. Euripides celebrated the ferocity of Agave and her fellow Maenads, Ino and Autonoë, in his *Bacchae* as soldiers reported how 'we by flight hardly escaped tearing to pieces at their hands' " and further described the shock of witnessing the semidivine females tearing young bulls limb from limb with their terrible "knifeless fingers." In Euripides' version, Pentheus dies while trying to spy on the private ritual of the Maenads in transvestite disguise.

- Admete, aka "the Untamed," bested Hercules and made him serve the goddess Hera. Hera rewarded Admete for her loyalty and excellence by appointing her head priestess of the island refuge Samos; Admete in turn honored her goddess with her evangelical fervor, expanding the territory of Hera's woman cult to the far reaches of the ancient world.

- Alcina made love to men and then turned them into inanimate objects once she had her pleasure.

- The harpies were daughters of Electra. They were predatory birds with the heads of women who were famous for stealing food away from a blind man. Aëllopus was the Harpy who fought the Argonauts; her name means "Storm-Foot."

- Scylla was a six-headed sea monster, and each head had three rows of sharp, pointed teeth. She lived in the Straits of Messina, where she devoured ships that came too close.

- Mermaids had women's bodies and fishlike tails. They would lure sailors to their deaths with their sweet songs.

- The Siren had a woman's body and a bird's wings, legs, and talons.

- The Sphinx had a woman's head and a lion's body.

- The Gorgons were three sisters who were clawed and winged monsters with live snakes for hair. Medusa, who killed Perseus, was the most famous.

The book *Sheroes* informs us that Norse mythology has a sort of class of afterlife Amazon warriors, the Valkyries, the "choosers of the slain" from Old Norse. Handmaidens of Odin, the Valkyries pick the most valiant warriors from among the slain on battlefields to be in the celestial army of the gods. In the Edda, the Valkyries include Gondul, "she wolf;" Skuld, "death-bringer;" Skorn; Brunnhilde, "she who calls out;" Hrist, "storm;" and Thrud, "force," who ride through the heavens on charging horses getting ready for Ragnarok, the battle marking the end of the world.

"The true measure of all our actions is how long the good in them lasts... everything we do, we do for the young."

—Queen Elizabeth II

CHAPTER 8

Women's Sporting Life

Gymnastics star Larissa Latynina, who competed in the Olympics in the 1960s, holds the record for the most medals (nine gold, five silver, and four bronze) of any Olympiad, as well as most individual medals and most medals by a woman.

Since the passage of Title IX in 1972, which was designed to create gender parity in athletics, statistics show a 7 percent increase in the ratio of female athletes in high school.

Total Knockouts

Hessie Donahue was just trying to be a good wife. So in 1892, when her husband, a boxing promoter, was at an exhibition in Arkansas promoting legendary fighter John L. Sullivan and there were no volunteers to do a little sparring, Hessie agreed to climb into the ring. However, John tagged Hessie's nose a little too hard. She got mad, hauled off, and belted him, and down he went for the count, making Hessie the only woman to ever knock out a major male boxing champion—at least in the ring.

Seventeen-year-old Jackie Mitchell pitched against the Yankees for the Chattanooga Lookouts in April 1931 in an exhibition game. She struck out both Babe Ruth and Lou Gehrig!

American Sharon Adams was a gung-ho sailor who in 1969 became the first woman to sail the Pacific solo.

Wilma Rudolph is a woman with the right stuff. Born with a disability that prevented her from walking until she was eight years old, she underwent hundreds of hours of physical therapy and began not only walking but also running. Turns out she was pretty good at it—at the age of twenty, she won three Olympic gold medals in track.

Grandmother Irene Horton, along with two of her children and three grandchildren, was a contender in the 1978 US Nationals in water-skiing.

In *Sheroes*, Varla Ventura relates the Greek myth of the first female Olympian, Atalanta of Boeotia.

> Born to Schoeneus, she cared not for weaving, the kitchen, or for wasting her precious time with any man who couldn't hold his own against her athletic prowess. Her father, proud of his fleet-footed Boeotian babe, disregarded the norms of ancient Greek society and didn't insist on marrying his daughter off for political or financial gain and supported her decision to marry the man who could outrun her. Her suitors were, however, given a head start, and Atalanta "armed with weapons pursues her naked suitor. If she catches him, he dies." She was outfoxed by Hippomenes who scattered golden apples as he ran, slowing down the Amazonian runner as she stopped to pick them up. Well matched in every way, they were happy together, even going so far as to desecrate a shrine to Aphrodite by making love on the altar! For this, the goddess turned Atalanta into a lioness, where she ruled yet again with her wild and regal spirit.

Actual Olympian Feats

According to Susan Wells in *The Olympic Spirit*, the original Greek games were "an exclusively male affair: no women were permitted, with the exception of the priestess of Demeter;

and according to the laws of Elis, any female who attempted to violate this taboo would be hurled to her certain death from a high, rocky cliff called the Tympaion. Fortunately, no female interlopers were ever caught—except for Kallipateira, who disguised herself as a male trainer to watch her son, Peisirodos, compete. When Peisirodos won his event, she jumped over a fence, uncovering her fraud in her excitement. Because Kallipateira's father, brothers, and son were all Olympic champions, her life was spared. But Olympic law was thereafter changed to require that all trainers, like athletes at the games, had to enter the arena without clothing."

Perturbed at being left out, women began to hold separate, women-only events known as the Heraean Games. Like the Olympics, they were held every four years in the Olympic stadium.

Eventually the gals were allowed into the real Olympics and often outshone the men in the equestrian events. Around 390 BC, the Spartan Cynisca, sister of King Agesilaus, led the all-female team that bested all the men in the chariot race; we know because a statue of her was erected with the other Olympians. And history records at least one other female chariot race champion, Belistiche of Macedonia.

When the modern Olympics were born in 1896, gold was considered inferior to silver, so first-place winners got silver medals. The switchover to gold (actually gold plate) happened in 1904.

In 1900, the Olympics were held in Paris. Instead of medals, the culture-loving French gave out artwork.

Olympic gold-medal figure skater Kristi Yamaguchi was born with clubfeet. As a child, she played with a Dorothy Hamill doll, which may have brought her luck, for she is the first American since Hamill to win the gold in figure skating.

Never Give Up

In 1912, golfer Maud McInnes was playing in a tournament when she hit her ball right into the river, where it floated away. Not one to be thwarted by such a minor inconvenience, Maud jumped into a rowboat, enlisting her husband to paddle. Eventually she drove the ball onto land and stroked her way back to the hole. It took two hours and 166 shots, but she did it.

Females Fore

One of the very first women golfers was Mary, Queen of Scots; her grandfather King James IV was the first person we know of who played the game.

In 1967, Renee Powell became the first African American woman on the Ladies' Professional Golf Association (LPGA) tour.

In 1926, miniature golf was invented by Tennessee entrepreneur Frieda Carter, part owner of the Fairyland Inn, who called it "Tom Thumb Golf" when she applied for a patent. The pastime grew by leaps and bounds; in 1930, there were 50,000 such courses nationwide.

Women didn't begin to play organized baseball until the 1860s, when women's colleges such as Vassar formed baseball clubs, despite public outcries that it was unladylike.

Most Valuable Player

"In her prime, she was so famous she was known simply as Babe," says *Hell's Belles* by Seale Ballenger.

That's because Texan Babe (real name Mildred) Didrikson Zaharias was one of the greatest natural athletes of all time. She could run, high jump, throw the javelin, play pool, swim, shoot some mean hoops, and swing a hot bat. A little wisp of a gal who stood just five foot four and barely weighed over a hundred pounds, she won the hearts of the American public by taking gold medals in the 80-meter hurdles and the javelin in the 1932 Olympics. And, as Charles McGrath points out in a 1996 profile in the *New York Times Magazine*, "She would have won the high jump, too, if the judges hadn't objected to her controversial technique of diving headfirst over the bar." (Asked at the time if there was anything she didn't play, she replied, "Yeah, dolls.")

And then there was her golf game. Determined to make money at athletics—times were different in the '30s, there were no big athletic shoe or cereal box contracts for Olympic stars and money was tight in her working-class family (as a junior high school student, Babe had worked in a fig-packing plant and later sewed potato sacks)—Babe decided to go where a woman could make money as an athlete and became a professional golfer. She applied her usual grit to succeeding, practicing until her hands were raw; she would often bandage them and continue on. While she perfected her technique, Babe kept body and soul together by various means, including playing on several women's baseball teams and doing vaudeville (she tumbled and played the harmonica).

Then she hit the women's golf circuit, dominating the sport throughout the '30s and '40s. She won seventeen straight amateur victories in one year, a record yet to be broken by either a man or woman, and won thirty-three pro tournaments, including three US Opens. She won the Associated Press's Woman Athlete of the Year five times and in 1950 was named the AP's Outstanding Woman Athlete of the Half Century.

Cofounder of the Ladies Pro Golf Association (LPGA) in 1949, she brought an athleticism to the sport that had for women been formerly characterized by elegant, but not very powerful shots. Babe wasn't concerned about being ladylike. "It's not enough to swing at the ball," she once said. "You've got to loosen your girdle and really let the ball have it." She often played in exhibition matches against men, and in 1951, she took up a challenge by British golf journalist Leonard Crawley, who, skeptical about the abilities of female pro golfers, bet Babe that she and her compadres couldn't beat the best six male amateur golfers in the world. If they did, Leonard would shave off his mustache. Babe, in typical belle fashion, rose to the challenge, and the women swept every match. Leonard, however, kept his mustache.

In 1938, she married wrestler George Zaharias, nicknamed "The Crying Greek from Cripple Creek" who managed her career. Perhaps her finest moment was in 1954, when she amazed the world by winning the US Open by twelve strokes, less than a year after undergoing major abdominal surgery for intestinal cancer. The cancer eventually stopped her however, and her death at the age of forty-three in 1956 was a huge loss for the sports world and all of America.

In 1976, the first year when women's basketball was an Olympic event, a Latvian by the name of Uljana Larionovna dominated the court. At seven-foot-two and 285 pounds, she averaged nineteen points a game and twelve rebounds, despite sitting on the bench for half of each game.

In 1984, Debi Thomas became the first African American ice skater on a World Team. Not only that, but she also went on to win the silver medal in the 1988 Winter Olympics, becoming the very first African American to take a medal at the event.

No Pressure Too Great

"Who alive in 1984 can forget the image of pixie-like Mary Lou Retton at the Summer Olympics?" writes Seale Ballenger in *Hell's Belles.*

Her lithesome body, perky good looks, and spunky spirit left an indelible mark on the American consciousness. (Plus, who could forget the face you saw for years on your Wheaties box?) Mary Lou was so popular that in 1993, nine years after the Olympics in which she had won five medals in gymnastics, including the gold for all around excellence, silver in team and vault, and bronze in uneven bars and floor exercise, she was still picked as the most popular female athlete in America (sharing the honors with ice skater Dorothy Hamill).

Mary Lou was born in a small coal mining town in West Virginia, the youngest of five. By age four, she was already enrolled in acrobatics and ballet classes, something her parents did because she was "very hyper." By seven, she was already training seriously; at eight, she saw Nadia Com neci in the Olympics and began to plan for her own equal success. At fifteen, she moved to

Houston to train with Bela Karolyi, the man who had coached Nadia, and began to win major prizes.

Just six weeks before she was to appear in the Olympics, she injured her knee and had to have arthroscopic surgery, but by competition time, she seemed to have totally recovered as she took to the arena and charmed the world. That year, in addition to her medals (and the Wheaties box), she was named Sports Illustrated Sportswoman of the Year and toured twenty-eight cities in the US, performing and appearing in parades. Still sought after for sports telecasting, product endorsements, and exhibitions, she lives in Houston, where she is married with children. She also gives inspirational speeches: "I tell people how to leave the comfort zone and meet life's challenges."

Tennis, Anyone?

Great Britain's Charlotte Cooper was the very first woman to win an Olympic event. It was for tennis, in 1900.

Martina Navratilova won nine Wimbledon's singles titles, the most of any woman, with Serena Williams and Steffi Graf following close behind her with seven Wimbledon wins each as of this writing.

The youngest woman to ever win at Wimbledon is Martina Hingis, who won in doubles in 1996, when she was fifteen.

Billie Jean King holds the record for most Wimbledon titles of any man or woman—twenty: six singles, ten doubles, and four mixed doubles.

Margaret Court of Australia won twenty-four Grand Slam singles titles in her heyday, three more than Steffi Graff.

Advice on Success from Two of the Best Tennis Pros in the World

"If you can react the same way to winning and losing, that…quality is important because it stays with you the rest of your life."

—Chris Evert

"I just concentrate on concentrating."

—Martina Navratilova

Althea Gibson was the first African American tennis player to make it big, winning back-to-back Wimbledon titles in 1957 and 1958, the French Open in 1956, and the US Championships in 1957 and 1958. She was also one of the pioneers of the LPGA, again breaking the color barrier as well as the gender barrier in professional golf. In her day, she received many honors— appearing on a Wheaties box and being given a parade down Broadway, to name just two—but never the kind of financial rewards later athletes reaped.

In the late 1990s, twin tennis sensations Venus and Serena Williams picked up where Gibson left off. Serena was the next black woman to win the US Open, in 1999, and Venus took the women's title at Wimbledon in 2000. Since then, the sisters have remained remarkably equal in their achievements; Serena has won seven major titles, and Venus six. Raised in a devout Jehovah's Witness family and homeschooled, the sisters are close friends despite having competed against each other for numerous major titles.

Men are more likely to get sports injuries than women, except in three sports—volleyball, bowling, and gymnastics. There, women lead the pack.

The very first woman to climb Mt. Everest was Junko Tabei of Japan, in 1975.

One woman athlete who was famous in the mid-twentieth century was Fanny Blaners-Koen. Known as "The Flying Dutchwoman," she dominated the track-and-field events at the 1948 Olympics, winning the sprint relay, the 80-meter hurdles, and the 100-meter and 200-meter dashes.

Golden Girl

Wyomia Tyus was stricken with polio and wore corrective shoes until she was ten. A mere eight years later, she won a gold medal in the 100-meter dash at the Tokyo Olympics. At the 1968 Mexico City Olympics, she became one of only two women at the time ever to win three gold medals and earned a place in the Olympic Hall of Fame. Her appearance in 1968 was controversial—militants had encouraged black athletes to boycott the games. Wyomia did not want to miss the opportunity of a lifetime, but she did wear black clothing in support.

German swimmer Hilde Schrader had a problem. Competing in the breaststroke at the 1928 Olympic Games, she swam so fast her bathing suit straps broke. "I would have gone even faster," she later confessed, "if I had not been so embarrassed." That's okay, Hilde, your time was fast enough to win the gold—and break the world record.

Lizzie Murphy was the first woman ever to play for a major league baseball team. In August 1922, she played first base for an all-star team in an exhibition game against the Red Sox—and Lizzie's team won.

The All-American Girls Baseball League

"For the briefest time in the 1940s, women had a 'league of their own,' " notes Varla Ventura in her book *Sheroes*.

And while it was not intended to be serious sports so much as a marketing package, the All-Girls Baseball League stormed the field and made it their own. The league was the brainchild of chewing gum magnate Phillip K. Wrigley, whose empire had afforded him the purchase of the Chicago Cubs. He came up with the concept of putting a bunch of sexy girls out on the field in short skirts and full makeup to entertain a baseball-starved population whose national pastime was put on hold as baseball players turned fighting men.

The players were eager to join these new teams called the Daisies, the Lassies, the Peaches, and the Belles because it was their only chance to play baseball professionally. Pepper Pair put it best in the book she and the other AAGBL players are profiled in, "You have to understand that we'd rather play ball than eat, and where else could we go and get paid a hundred dollars a week to play ball?" After the war, men returned home and major league baseball was revived. However the All-Girls League hung on, even spawning the rival National Girl's Baseball League. With more opportunity for everyone, teams suddenly had to pay more money to their best players in order to hang on to them and both leagues attracted players from all around the US and Canada....

Ironically, the television boom of the fifties eroded the audience for the AAGBL as well as many other semi-pro sports. The death blow to the women's baseball leagues came, however, with the creation of the boys-only Little League. Girls no longer had a way to develop their skills in their youth and were back to sandlots and cornfields, and the AAGBL died in 1954.

CHAPTER 9

Celebrity Sightings of the Female Variety

Joan Crawford was scheduled to be the lead in *From Here to Eternity* but refused the role after she saw the costumes. Deborah Kerr was then cast and went on to be tapped for an Oscar for the part.

Those in the know tell us that Crawford had a real rivalry going with Marilyn Monroe. Ms. Joan got mad because she felt Marilyn's low-cut gown had upstaged her at some celebrity event, declaring loudly that she had tits too.

"Faye Dunaway rocketed to international fame," notes *Hell's Belles*, when the green-eyed epitome of the Southern belle portrayed Bonnie Parker in the 1967 Arthur Penn movie *Bonnie and Clyde*, a film that "marked the turn from Western to Southern settings in popular adventure dramas," according to *The Encyclopedia of Southern Culture*.

An "army brat" and a native of Bascom, Florida, Faye Dunaway was nominated for an Academy Award for her performance. Her career flourished with roles in *Chinatown* (earning another nomination) and Paddy Chayefsky's brilliant *Network*, for which she won the Academy's Best Actress award in 1976. In her long and luminous career, Dunaway is perhaps best remembered for her all-hells-broken-loose portrayal of film legend Joan Crawford in *Mommy Dearest* (1981). In that role, the bellicose belle called upon her Southern strength and iron will, bursting forward with the unforgettable declaration that became a mantra of the '80s, "No more wire hangers!" And who could forget the sight of Faye-as-Joan when she shrieked these immortal lines at a PepsiCo board of directors meeting after the death of her husband: "Don't f*** with me fellas, it's not my first trip to the rodeo!"

♥♥ ♥♥ ♥♥

Jennifer Aniston almost missed her chance for a role in *The Breakup* because producers thought it insensitive to ask her so soon after her infamous split with Brad Pitt.

Diane Keaton and director Woody Allen have made eight movies together: *Play It Again, Sam* (1972), *Sleeper* (1973), *Love and Death* (1975), *Annie Hall* (1977), *Interiors* (1978), *Manhattan* (1979), *Radio Days* (1987), and *Manhattan Murder Mystery* (1993).

Ignominious Beginnings

Madonna once worked at a Dunkin' Donuts in New York. She was fired, however, for squirting a customer with jelly.

Roseanne was once fired too—from her job as a salad lady at Chuckarama in Salt Lake City. She had been to the dentist and wasn't feeling well and refused to go into the walk-in freezer.

Did you know that Bette Midler's first job was as a pineapple chunker, presumably in a canning factory?

Cyndi Lauper's first gig was as a dog-kennel cleaner.

The singer Dusty Springfield had her career as a salesclerk short-circuited. She was fired from Bentalls' for accidentally blowing the store's lighting system.

Judy Garland got her big break in 1936 because someone didn't hear correctly. She was fourteen and was appearing with fifteen-year-old Deanna Durbin in a short film. Louis B. Mayer, the head of MGM, told his assistant to sign up the flat one (referring to Durbin, who had a tendency to go off key). The hapless helper thought he said, "Fat one," referring to Garland.

A beautiful girl named Norma Jean was working in an aircraft factory during WWII when an army photographer showed up to take pictures for propaganda purposes and recommended her to a modeling agency. Within months, she had reincarnated as Marilyn Monroe.

What was the original name of the band Blondie? The Stilettos.

Lata Mangeshker was one busy singer. In thirty years, she recorded approximately 25,000 songs in twenty Indian languages and sang in over 1,800 movies.

James Bondage

- Number of women in James Bond films and books: 54
- Number of women killed in James Bonds films and books: 48
- Number of women killed by James Bond himself: 11
- Number of women James Bond slept with in books or films: 45
- Number of women in James Bond films or movies that he has not slept with: 9

Who are they? Gala Brand, Tilly Masterson, Loelia Pononby, Maria Freudenstein, May Jane Mashkin, Rhonda Llewellyn Masters, Heather Dare, Miss Moneypenny, and Clover Pennington.

The most popular women's magazine in the world is *Cosmopolitan*.

Lucille Ball was on the cover of the very first *TV Guide*. Since then, she has been on more *TV Guide* covers than anyone.

It's Not Nice to Fool People

Two drive-time radio jocks got fired from their station for perpetrating a hoax that Britney Spears had been killed in an auto accident.

"I like to wake up feeling
a new man."

—Jean Harlow, to a reporter who
inquired about her morning routine

"There are breast roles and there are non-breast roles. For instance, when I was Stella in A Streetcar Named Desire on Broadway in 1988, I thought they were appropriate."

—Frances McDormand

"Here, hold my tits for me, will ya?"

—Ann Sheridan, removing her falsies (they were heavy rubber in those days)

"I thought it was awfully messy."

—Jean Harlow about her first
sexual experience

"His idea of a romantic kiss was to go 'Blaaah' and gag me with his tongue. He only improved once he married Demi Moore."

—Cybill Shepherd, on Bruce Willis

"In Europe, it doesn't matter if you're a man or a woman; we make love to anyone we find attractive."

—Marlene Dietrich

"Just imagine, I'm in bed with Jimmy Cagney!"

—Merle Oberon, who was not known for discretion

"My father warned me about men and booze, but he never mentioned a word about women and cocaine."

—Tallulah Bankhead

"On location...he wasn't a good kisser. Then we came to London and...he was wonderful—I couldn't understand it. It turned out that his wife was with him in London. He was much looser when she was there."

—Cybill Shepherd, on Michael Caine

♥♥ ♥♥ ♥♥

Live theater has its origins in ancient hunting and fertility rituals. By the time of the Pharaohs, the Egyptians were putting on religious plays, with priests acting out the story of Osiris.

Actress Adah Menken was the first actress to appear nude (or at least mostly). It was 1864, and she was playing a part in which she was tied to the back of a wild horse by a rampaging Cossack.

The concept for repertory theater—a building with a permanent cast—was the brainchild of Annie Elizabeth Fredericka Horniman, who established the Abbey Theatre in Dublin in 1904. She was the first person to stage the famous play by George Bernard Shaw, *Arms and the Man*.

The Pens of Protégées

Who says you need experience to write? Many girls have picked up pens at a very young age and have written books that have found critical and popular acclaim. The most famous, of course, is Anne Frank, who kept a diary as a teenager in hiding from the Nazis during WWII. *The Diary of Anne Frank* has now been published in over fifty languages and is read by children and teenagers everywhere. But she is not the only one:

- S. E. Hinton began writing *The Outsiders* when she was only fifteen. Her story of teenage gangs, published when she was seventeen, has sold over one million copies in the United States alone.

- Maghanita Kempadoo was only twelve when she wrote a parody of "The Twelve Days of Christmas" entitled *Letter of Thanks*. It was published in 1969.

- Then there's Dorothy Straight, who wrote *How the World Began* at age four. It was published by the time she was six.

- Three of the famed Brontë sisters were writers from the time they could pick up a pen. Creating imaginary lands, they wrote short stories, poetry, and scripts that they performed for their reclusive father.

In the early days of motion pictures, Marguerite Clark was Mary Pickford's biggest rival for the title of "America's Sweetheart." Then she married Harry Palmerston-Williams, who insisted that she have a no-kissing clause in her contract. Immediately her popularity plummeted, and her career was over.

Precocious Musical Ears

Opera conductor and producer Sarah Caldwell was recognized as a mathematical and musical prodigy by the time she was four. At sixteen, she had her own radio show on which she performed. At twenty-nine, she founded the Opera Company of Boston with five thousand dollars in 1958.

Russian Olya Zaranika was the ripe old age of seven when she wrote her second opera and nine when her first opera was staged—in the Russian capital no less.

Trinidad native Hazel Scott was a musical protégé who lived in the early part of the twentieth century. She began playing the piano at the age of three. At eight, she was given a scholarship to the Juilliard School of Music, even though they had a rule that you had to be sixteen to gain admission. As an adult, she sang, acted, and performed classical music and died at age sixty-one.

Both Carole King and Rita Coolidge not only wrote songs but also had songs written about them. Neil Sedaka wrote "Oh Carol"—and Carol wrote "Oh Neil" in response, while Joe Cocker penned "Delta Lady" for Rita.

Billy Joel wrote his hit song "Uptown Girl" for his then-wife, Christie Brinkley.

I always thought Carly Simon wrote "You're So Vain" about Mick Jagger and then had him sing backup as irony upon irony. But after intense media speculation about whom she did have in mind, she finally said, "There is nothing in the lyric which isn't true of Warren Beatty."

Tinsel Town Tidbits

Kim Basinger made a CD called *The Color of Sex.*

Loretta Young got her break when a director called looking for her sister Polly Ann, a minor star. Polly wasn't home, but the fifteen-year-old Loretta talked her way into a movie career.

To keep up her sexy image, Jean Harlow would ice her nipples just before the cameras rolled.

Marlene Dietrich has the distinction of being one of the most famous insomniacs of all times.

Emma Thompson credits her glowing complexion in *Howard's End* to her tight corset, which made all her blood rush to her face.

Joan Crawford extracted her back teeth to make her cheeks cave in and heighten her cheekbones.

Rumor has it that Jane Fonda had a rib removed to give herself a smaller waist.

At one point in Joan Crawford's career, her contract specified what time she had to go to bed each night.

Take that! Once a drunk restaurant-goer dared to call Lena Horne the "N" word. She (understandably) responded by throwing a lamp, an ashtray, and several drinking glasses.

Forties starlet Marie McDonald was more known for her seven marriages than for her B-grade movies. The reason, she said, was that "husbands are easier to find than good agents."

Ever notice that actress Meryl Streep is rarely filmed head-on? It's because she was born with a deviated septum, which she refuses to have fixed.

Several famous females are known by their middle names. They include:

- Dorothy Faye Dunaway

- Helen Beatrix Potter

- Ernestine Jane Geraldine Russell

- Edith Norma Shearer

- Marie Dionne Warwick

- Marie Debra Winger

At least five big female movie stars got their start in soaps.

1. Patty Duke, in *The Brighter Day*

2. Mia Farrow, in *Peyton Place*

3. Susan Sarandon, in *A World Apart* and *Search for Tomorrow*

4. Kathleen Turner, in *The Doctors*

5. Sigourney Weaver, in *Somerset*

The Glamorous Gabors

The famous Gabor sisters—Zsa Zsa, Eva, and Magda—loved to be coy about their ages. At one point in her life, Zsa Zsa produced a birth certificate that said she was born in 1928, which would have meant she had married her first husband at age eight and married her second husband, the famous hotelier Conrad Hilton, at fourteen. When someone astute at math pointed this out to her, she said, "Conrad made me promise to never, never reveal my true age. And I haven't." All three sisters were equally secretive about their ages; Eva's tombstone only gives her date of death, not birth. The famous gossip columnist Cindy Adams wrote of them: "I used to say that the only way you could tell the true age of a Gabor was by the rings around their gums."

Between them, the much-marrying three sisters had twenty husbands.

Zsa Zsa and Eva looked so alike that even those who knew them well confused them. Once, when Eva was caught swimming nude in her pool by a telephone repairman, she pretended to be Zsa Zsa.

Critics consider Sappho to be the greatest ancient poet. While her work, like that of all the poets of the time, was oral, it was later recorded in nine books of lyric poetry and one of elegiac verse. During the Middle Ages, however, the Catholic Church deemed her work to be obscene, so they burned the volume containing her complete body of work, leaving only a few poems for today's audience. Scholars, however, continue to scour old libraries in search of another copy.

Thirties star Vivienne Segal was also a boxing fan. Her contract specified that she could not yell during fights so as to not injure her vocal cords.

Unsung Heroine

Germaine de Staël was the foremost female intellectual of the Romantic period. Her forward-thinking parents taught her to read and write, skills possessed by very few women of the 1700s.

Writes Becca Anderson in *The Book of Awesome Women Writers*,

> In 1786, she married the baron de Staël-Holstein, ambassador of Sweden. Their marriage was tumultuous, and she took many lovers, most notably Romantic August Schlegel and Benjamin Constant, a writer with liberation politics who became her longtime companion. In Paris, Madame de Staël formed a salon, a hotbed of politics and culture. She invited new and established writers, artists, and thinkers alike.
>
> Her praise of the German state prompted Napoleon to banish her from France. She picked up her life and moved to an estate she maintained in Switzerland at Coppet on Lake Geneva where she created another and equally dazzling group of cerebral companions, including Rousseau, Byron, and Shelly.
>
> As a writer, de Staël greatly influenced Europe of the day with her cardinal work *On Germany*, as well as her novels *Delphine* and *Corinne*, a nonfiction sociological study of

literature, and her memoir, *Ten Years of Exile*, published in 1818.

Corinne is her best-loved work, a daring story of an affair between a brilliant Italian woman and an English noble that explores themes of purity, free love, the place of domesticity, Italian art, architecture, geography, politics, and woman as genius as seen through the Romantic lens. At this writing there is no English translation of *Corinne* in print, and prior to the last one, there had been no new translation of the novel in nearly a hundred years, despite de Staël's status as one of the preeminent women of letters of all time.

Most schoolchildren are taught that Harriet Beecher Stowe was an extremely creative young woman who almost accidentally wrote a book that tore America apart. The truth is that *Uncle Tom's Cabin* was written with precisely the intent of publicizing the cruelty of slavery and galvanizing people to act. It came as no surprise when her book was banned in the South as subversive. (It still makes lists of banned books today.)

Did you know that poet and performer Maya Angelou, one of the greatest voices of our times, spent five years totally mute? Maya was raised predominantly by her grandmother. When she was seven, while on a visit to her mother, she was raped by her mother's boyfriend, which she reported to her mother. The man was tried and sent to jail, which confused and upset the young girl. When he was killed in prison for being a child molester, she felt responsible and stopped speaking.

Most of us know that Candice Bergen is the daughter of the ventriloquist Edgar Bergen, whose famous dummy was Charlie McCarthy. But did you know that when Candice was young, her room was smaller than Charlie's and she had fewer clothes than he did?

Sherry Lansing, the actress who played opposite John Wayne in the 1970 film *Rio Lobo*, became Twentieth Century Fox's vice president of production ten years later.

When she was first starting out, child star Shirley Temple had an insurance policy with an exemption that no money would be paid if she were hurt or killed while drunk.

The story of Cinderella has been made into more movies than any other tale.

Banned in Boston—Or Elsewhere

Books continue to be challenged, burned, or banned. Here's a list of titles by women that have received such treatment somewhere in the United States in the past few decades. Judy Blume holds the distinction of appearing five times.

- *Beloved* by Toni Morrison

- *Blubber* by Judy Blume

- *Bridge to Terabithia* by Katherine Paterson

- *Changing Bodies, Changing Lives* by Ruth Bell

- *The Clan of the Cave Bear* by Jean Auel

- *The Color Purple* by Alice Walker

- *Diary of a Young Girl* by Anne Frank

- *Flowers in the Attic* by V. C. Andrews

- *Forever* by Judy Blume

- *Gigi's House* by Judy Blume

- *The Great Gilly Hopkins* by Katherine Paterson

- *The Handmaid's Tale* by Margaret Atwood
- *Harriet the Spy* by Louise Fitzhugh
- *The Headless Cupid* by Zilpha Keatley Snyder
- *Heather Has Two Mommies* by Lesléa Newman
- *I Know Why the Caged Bird Sings* by Maya Angelou
- *It's Okay If You Don't Love Me* by Norma Klein
- *The Joy Luck Club* by Amy Tan
- *Little House in the Big Woods* by Laura Ingalls Wilder
- *Love Is One of the Choices* by Norma Klein
- *My Friend Flicka* by Mary O'Hara
- *My House* by Nikki Giovanni
- *On My Honor* by Marion Dane Bauer
- *Ordinary People* by Judith Guest
- *Silas Marner* by George Eliot
- *Superfudge* by Judy Blume
- *Then Again, Maybe I Won't* by Judy Blume
- *Uncle Tom's Cabin* by Harriet Beecher Stowe
- *A Wrinkle in Time* by Madeleine L'Engle

Only five women directors have so far been nominated for an Academy Award: Greta Gerwig for *Lady Bird* (2017), Kathryn Bigelow for *The Hurt Locker* (2008), Sofia Coppola for *Lost in Translation* (2003), Jane Campion for *The Piano* (1993), and Lina Wertmuller for *Seven Beauties* (1976); this has given rise to the hashtags #FemaleDirectors and #OscarsSoMale.

Novelist Jackie Collins, well known for her sex scenes, actually got her start as a writer of sex scenes at age eleven by selling classmates peeks into her supposedly true diary. "Of course, I didn't know what the hell I was talking about until I was at least, um, thirteen."

It's hard to believe today because Jane Austen is now beloved by readers everywhere and regarded as one of the true masters of the English novel, but she received little critical or popular attention during her lifetime. Indeed, she spent twenty-five years writing novels that were not even published under her name. It was only after her death at age forty-one that her books began to identify their author.

No women have speaking parts in the epic movie *Lawrence of Arabia*.

"Margaret Mitchell never intended to publish *Gone with the Wind*," notes *The Book of Awesome Women Writers*:

> She began writing her epic novel in 1926 as a private exercise after a serious ankle injury ended her brief career as a columnist for the *Atlanta Journal*. The manuscript evolved over a period of ten years into a massive cluttered stack of disjointed papers. She rarely spoke about it to anyone, although after a while the existence of this huge pile of words became common knowledge among her friends, one of whom was MacMillian editor Harold Latham, who in a 1935 visit to Atlanta, asked Margaret if he could take a look at it.
>
> Impulsively, and in retrospect, surprisingly for someone who considered herself a poor writer and was extremely private about her writing, Margaret bundled up the huge stack of handwritten pages and dumped them onto his lap. Almost immediately she had second thoughts, and when Harold got back to New York, he found a telegram informing him that she had changed her mind and to send the

manuscript back. By then, he had already become ensnared in the saga (even though at the time it lacked a first chapter and any semblance of order).

Dolores Hart was a starlet who appeared in many '50s movies, including *Loving You* with Elvis Presley. In the early '60s, however, she set Hollywood agog by becoming a nun. She's still in the convent today.

Women Who Loved Writing So Much They Hid Their Gender to Get Published

- Amandine Lucie Aurore Dupin, Baronne Dudevant: an aristocratic lady who wrote as the famous French novelist George Sand

- Mary Ann (or Marian) Evans: the real name of the great English Victorian novelist George Eliot

- Acton, Currer, and Ellias Bell: the beloved Brontës; Ann, Charlotte, and Emily, respectively

- Lee Chapman, John Dexter, and Morgan Ives: all noms de plume of Marion Zimmer Bradley, author of *The Mists of Avalon*

- Ralph Iron: the name Olive Schreiner used to write her acclaimed *The Story of an African Farm*

- Frank: the name the first woman humorist in the United States, Frances Miriam Berry Witcher, used to get published

🐦 Lawrence Hope: the pseudonym of Adele Florence Cory, a woman who, according to *Womanlist* by Marjorie P. K. Weiser and Jean S. Arbeiter, was "respectably married to a middle-aged British Army officer in India; [she] wrote passionate poems in the 1890s. One described the doomed love of a married English lady for an Indian rajah in the Kasmir. When Hope's real identity was unmasked, all London was abuzz: Was she telling the truth?"

💜💜 💜💜 💜💜

Lupe Velez, the 1940s film star nicknamed the Mexican Spitfire, was reputed to have a particular talent—she could spin her left breast clockwise or counterclockwise while the right remained still.

Lovely Jailbirds

In 1978, Jane Russell was imprisoned for driving while intoxicated. Sophia Loren went to jail for a while, too, in 1982, for tax "irregularities."

The Eyes Have It

Demi Moore was born cross-eyed, while Jane Seymour has one green eye and one brown. And Rita Hayworth had one eye significantly larger than the other, a flaw she covered up with special eyelashes.

Pioneering gossip writer Elizabeth Keckley was born a slave, but she went on to become one of history's first gossip writers. She bought her freedom with her skills as a dressmaker. In 1855, she moved to Baltimore, where she started a school for black girls, teaching sewing and etiquette. From there she moved to Washington, DC, where she came to the attention of First Lady Mary Todd Lincoln. Elizabeth became Mary's dressmaker and eventually her close friend. She was one of the few people who could tolerate Mary's sharp tongue and unstable personality. But the friendship was put to the test, and failed, when Elizabeth printed *Behind the Scenes: Thirty Years a Slave* and *Four Years in the White House*, a book that included many details about life in the White House.

Mary Todd Lincoln had been criticized for years for her love of expensive clothes, furs, and jewelry. She was called pretentious and extravagant, criticisms that increased after her husband's death. Elizabeth, one of Mary's closest friends, knew she was impulsive, ambitious, and insecure, but she also knew that she was loving and charitable. She wrote *Behind the Scenes* intending to support her friend and help set the record straight, but her perceived betrayal of confidences created an irreparable rift in the relationship. They never spoke again.

Katherine Hepburn suffered from a phobia of dirty hair. When she was shooting at Twentieth Century Fox, she would sniff the heads of the cast and crew to make sure their hair was squeaky clean.

Hedy Lamarr had her autobiography, *Ecstasy and Me*, penned by ghostwriters. Apparently, however, she didn't ever look at it, at least not until after it was published and causing a stir. It was so full of juicy details that she ended up suing her own ghost.

Dawn Powell was a contemporary of Dreiser, Hemingway, and Dos Passos who could drink them under the table and hold her own in hard living as well as in her output of fifteen slightly shocking novels. Her titles alone—*The Wicked Pavilion, The Locusts Have No King, Angels on Toast*—evince creativity and cheek, but they quickly slid out of print. Recently, however, she has been rescued from obscurity and her books are once again becoming available.

Profile of Patsy

"There is just something about Patsy Cline that the American imagination won't let go of. Perhaps it was her death in a tragic plane crash at the age of thirty. Or maybe it was her unbridled sexuality, consummate confidence, and foul mouth during a time when women weren't supposed to say such things," writes Seale Ballenger in *Hell's Belles*.

"She had a mouth like a sailor, and she didn't put on airs. She was just Patsy, comfortable in her skin. I admired that," remembers Vivian Liberto, first wife of singer Johnny Cash, in a profile of Patsy for the *New York Times Magazine*.

Born Virginia Patterson Henley in 1932, her first idol was Shirley Temple, but her peripatetic family could not afford the singing or dancing lessons she begged for. By the time she was ten, she was determined to become a country music singer despite a difficult home life—her parents were constantly breaking up, and Patsy once hinted at sexual abuse by her father. A bout with rheumatic fever at age thirteen left her with "a booming voice like Kate Smith," said Patsy in a 1957 interview. When times got tough for her family, the feisty fourteen-year-old, passing for sixteen, went to work at a poultry factory plucking chickens, and later went to work at a drugstore.

But she was more determined than ever to make it, spending every available hour singing at parties, church socials, and the like, protecting herself from men who got too close. "Nothing men do surprises me," she once said. "I'm ready for them. I know how to whack below the belt." She did take help when offered, though. In 1952, she met Bill Peer, who gave her the first stage name she used, Patsy Hensley, got her the first gigs of her career, and fell head over heels in love with her. Patsy didn't reciprocate his affections completely. In the middle of their torrid love affair, she married Gerald Cline, juggling the two of them (plus a few other beaus) as well as a burgeoning career in Nashville. She got her big break in 1957, winning the Arthur Godfrey Talent Scout contest at the age of twenty-four performing the classic "Walkin' After Midnight." Over the next six years, she became the first female country and western singer ever to cross over successfully on both.

CHAPTER 10

Final Feminine Facts You Absolutely Can't Live Without

Ninety percent of all Hallmark cards are bought by women.

More people spend time in casinos than any other recreational venue.

When in the casino, women are twice as likely to play the slot machines or roulette than men, while men play more craps than women.

Every year, each person living in the United States uses things made from wood equal to a hundred-foot-tall tree.

Given our population, that works out to a forest of over 300 million trees in one year!

Wacky Laws for Humans

Don't fall asleep in the bathtub in Detroit. You could be arrested.

Don't try to buy peanuts after sundown in Alabama. It's illegal.

And my personal favorite: Never hang men's and women's underwear together on the clothesline in Minnesota, or you'll face stiff penalties.

Kaycee Nicole Swenson was a high school basketball player who documented her fight against leukemia on a website. Many people tracked her progress for over a year. Finally, one day, rather than a diary entry, there was a notice that she had passed away. Visitors to her website grieved for her. Shortly thereafter, it was revealed that the whole thing was a hoax made up by a mother of two in Kansas. The woman who created the story didn't have much to say about why she did it except that "she wanted it to be something positive," wrote Jon Carroll in the *San Francisco Chronicle*.

According to scientists, roses do not have thorns. They have prickles. Here's the difference: Thorns modify branches (and therefore are hard to break off), while prickles are outgrowths of the stem's skin (and therefore easy to break off). Either way, they are no fun.

The longest will ever written was the one written by Mrs. Frederica Cook, who wrote a will of 100,000 words bound into four volumes. Precisely what it all said is unclear.

Ancient Oddities

There were no specific names for girls in ancient Rome. Girls were given boys' names with an *a, ina,* or *ia* on the end: Theodora, Agrippina, Octavia.

In Greece of old, there were special "women's police" whose job it was to make sure women were where they were supposed to be and doing only what they were supposed to be doing.

When the phone company first started giving out the time, there were no such things as tape recorders. Real live women would have to say, "10 a.m. and 10 seconds, 10 a.m. and 14 seconds," all throughout the day and night. According to *Know It All!*, it was such a tedious job that no one could do it for more than a half hour at a stretch. Then they would have to take a rest.

Of Moms and Apple Pie

We in the United States spend about twenty-seven dollars apiece on our mothers for Mother's Day.

The notorious gangster Al Capone could not talk to his mother when she visited him in prison. Only English was allowed, and she spoke only Italian.

73 percent of mothers in the United States work outside the home, and 61 percent of those use childcare in some form.

In a survey of mothers and grandmothers in *Child* magazine, 91 percent of mothers felt they are as good as or better mothers than their mothers.

Eighty percent of grandmothers in the *Child* survey believe their grandchildren's mothers are doing an excellent job, and 20 percent even admitted that they were less than stellar moms in their day.

It's not such a lovefest when it comes to in-laws. Only 22 percent of daughters feel their mothers give them too much unwanted advice, compared to 55 percent who feel their mothers-in-law do.

Thirty-nine percent of daughters-in-law believe mothers-in-law don't understand how the world has changed since they were parents, and 60 percent who live near their mothers-in-law say she is too critical of how they discipline their kids.

Whistler only painted the famous portrait of his mother because his model failed to show up one day.

Can't Get No Respect: No, there is no official Mother-in-Law Day. The House passed a law in 1981 establishing such an event, but the Senate never did, so it doesn't really exist. Despite that fact, 800,000 folks send Mother-in-Law cards on the day the House designated—the fourth Sunday in October.

The average mother changes her baby's diapers 10,000 times before the child is potty trained (unless she has some help from Dad).

The oldest mother on record with a natural birth (rather than one that used some kind of fertility method) is Welsh farmer Elizabeth Buttle, who had a baby in 1998 at the age of sixty.

The use of surrogate mothers goes back to ancient Rome, where childless couples would seek out a woman willing to have sex with the husband and give the couple the child.

Because on average women live longer than men, you have an 11 percent chance of your mother coming to live with you at some point in her old age, as opposed to a 6 percent chance of your dad's arrival on your doorstep.

Rah! Rah! Sis Boom Bah! My Mom Tried to Kill Your Mom! Ha! Ha!

"Who can forget Wanda Webb Holloway, the Channelview, Texas, housewife convicted in 1991 of murder for hire?" writes Seale Ballenger in *Hell's Belles*.

> She was just trying to be a good mother to her eighth-grade daughter, Shanna Harper, who was trying out for the school's cheerleading squad and was facing stiff competition in Amber Heath, a classmate who had gotten a spot on the squad two years in a row. Wanda had the bright idea that if she could have Amber's mother, Verna, "taken care of," the girl would be so grief-stricken that she would drop out of

cheerleading, assuring her daughter of not only the plum cheerleading spot, but all the attendant friends and dates that come with it.

So she hired and conspired with a hit man, actually her ex-brother-in-law, even giving him a pair of diamond earrings as a down payment. But the police got wind of the scheme before it could be carried out and it was off to the pokey for the so-called Cheerleader Mom. In 1991, she was tried and sentenced to fifteen years in prison and fined $10,000. But there was a snafu—a juror was later discovered to have been on probation and so Wanda's conviction was overturned. In 1996, as a second trial was about to take place, she pleaded no contest and received a ten-year sentence....

Wanda did not spend much time in prison. In February, 1997, Judge George Godwin ruled that she would not benefit from any more prison time (she had served six months) and released her, under the condition that she perform a thousand hours of community service as penance.

The cheerleading misadventures stirred up a whirlwind of tabloid fodder and at least two made for television movies, including Holly Hunter's portrayal of Wanda in HBO's *The Positively True Adventures of the Texas Cheerleader Mom*. And what ever happened to the battling junior belles? Back in 1991, with the murder plot foiled, both girls again tried out for the squad. Popular Amber made it for the third year in a row, while sinister Wanda's little Shanna was rejected, once again.

Another notorious mother was Kate Barker, popularly called "Ma Barker." She was the mom and ringleader of the Barker Brothers, four notorious gangsters of the 1930s. It was her planning that enabled them to pull off a series of bank heists and post office robberies. She was also the mastermind behind the kidnapping of millionaire William Hamm, whom the gang successfully ransomed for $100,000. But her luck eventually ran out. She and one of her sons were gunned down by the FBI in a shoot-out in 1935.

Give Me That Remote!

When the TV is on, men are in charge of the remote control 55 percent of the time. Men channel surf way more than women do as well—85 percent of men can't stay with one channel versus 60 percent of females. And because they love channel surfing, they complain less about someone else doing it than women do—66 percent less.

A long-term study on the resilience of seven hundred women and men by Emmy E. Werner and her associates at the University of California at Davis found that nine out of ten women (as compared to seven out of ten men) relied on one or two long-term close friends when times got tough.

Forty percent of those surveyed say most of their family conversations happen in the living room, despite homebuilders' stories that living rooms are dead.

Recently, one of the last three Dionne quintuplets died, bringing attention once again to their infamous story. When the Dionnes were born in 1934 in Ontario, Canada, they were the first quintuplets ever to survive. Soon the government decided that their parents were unfit and removed the five to a hospital they constructed just for them. Known as Quintland, it soon became a major tourist attraction and moneymaker for the Ontario government during the Depression. Over five million folks paid to view the quints through a glass window. As adults, the five sued the government for their treatment and were awarded $2.8 million. They were not a long-lived bunch. The first sister died at twenty, the second at thirty-four, the third at sixty-seven.

The average woman in the United States spends almost one-third of her food budget on restaurants and takeout food.

When buying computers, cell phones, and other electronics, men are more likely to read the brochures and leave without talking to a salesperson. So says Paco Underhill in *Why We Buy*. Women tend to speak to sales personnel, preferring to get their information from a person rather than a piece of paper. Both require several trips to the store for a technological purchase, with women averaging one more than men. Electronics purchases differ in one other way—here men are the browsers, women are the "get the right thing and get out" types. Women are in the electronics store to buy, not to moon over the latest scanner. Ditto for Web buying. Internet sites are discovering that women log on, go to their destination, and purchase; men are the ones who flit from here to there.

Included among the more interesting beauty pageant titles women can aspire to are:

- Miss Crustacean USA
- Miss Muskrat
- Miss Swamp Cabbage Queen

Half of all *People* magazines sold at the checkout stand are impulse purchases, depending on who's on the cover. Who's the most popular cover subject ever? Princess Di, of course.

In the Car

Male drivers have more car accidents than female drivers, but they also drive more. If you calculate accidents per miles driven, women come out on top.

However, a male driver is 25 percent more likely to kill you in an accident than a female driver.

A sixteen-year-old boy driver is forty times more dangerous than a forty-year-old woman.

Don't gloat yet—as women age, they become as dangerous as teenage boys behind the wheel.

According to *Danger Ahead*, at many gas stations the regular and premium pumps actually are connected to the same tank. Tsk, tsk!

Coming up with the safest color cars to ride in turns out to be dependent on when you drive. Blue cars are safest in the day, yellow at night. If you want to hedge your bets overall, try white.

Lucky Vesna Vulovic was a flight attendant on an ill-fated flight in 1972. Her aircraft exploded and she fell 33,300 feet, landing in a snowbank. She suffered a leg injury; the twenty-seven other people on the flight all died.

Mars and Venus Go to Preschool

Studying gender differences in very young children, British researchers Diane McGuiness and Corinne Hutt discovered that:

- Girls as young as two or three days old maintain eye contact twice as long as boys.

- Preschool girls spend on average one and a half minutes saying good-bye to their mothers when they are being dropped off; boys spend about thirty seconds.

- A new kid at school, regardless of gender, tends to be ignored by the boys and approached with friendliness by the girls.

Who needed a study to tell us that women make three times as many personal phone calls as men and their conversations last around twenty minutes per call? Men on the other hand, when they do make calls, only speak for six minutes or so. Just keeping our relationships going...

Although women are more likely than men to remember to turn on the outside lights before they leave the house for the evening, they are less likely to lock their doors! Not a good idea for our physical safety.

The Smiles Have It

- Women smile more than men.

- Women, more than men, often smile from nervousness—from a desire to be liked and a fear that they won't be.

- Women tend to smile at people they know, whereas men feel more comfortable smiling at strangers on the street. (They don't have to worry as much about how such a smile might be construed.)

- Women tend to smile while delivering bad news, some so much that the point of their message is unclear.

And They Say We're the Fickle Ones

Researchers at Northwestern University want us to know that men change their minds two to three times more than women. On the other hand, women take longer to make up our minds, but once we do, we tend to stick to our decisions.

Women take up less space when talking than men, moving only their head, feet, and hands. Men, on the other hand, tend to use more whole movements and wider positions.

AFTERWORD

Hi there!

If you're reading this, I hope you enjoyed the world of new facts, quirky truths, and incredible feats *all* accomplished by the plethora of amazing women listed in this book! My name is Becca Anderson, and I'm honored to be adding the epilogue to this fascinating volume. Growing up on a farm in Ohio, I was raised by a handful of strong women who (though they may have not received the trivia-book recognition they deserved) were some of the smartest, funniest, and most inspiring people I have met to this day. Each of these women equipped me with various vital tools to tackle the journey of life: a love of gardening, compassion, intellect, and humor, to only name a few. Most notably, my first grade teacher, Mrs. Knowles, bestowed upon me her love of literature. Each week, Mrs. Knowles would hand me a new novel, checking in on my progress and recommending me a new read when she sensed I was nearly done with the last. We maintained this tight relationship for years beyond my elementary school career; time to time we still shoot one another book recommendations over email! More than just introducing me to incredible novels and even more extraordinary authors, Mrs. Knowles's gestures of kindness and care lit a spark in me to seek out genuine female empowerment and connection. To pay it forward, I've dedicated my career to children as well, teaching grade-school kids everything from English to multiplication, but *most* importantly kindness and compassion. I practice what I preach in my day-to-day routine as well, showing love to Mother Earth with my love of gardening and landscaping.

I believe each and every woman on this beautiful planet is capable of amazing feats—some utterly breathtaking and others simply quirky and fun. *Everything* should be celebrated, and that's why I love this book! Although we live in an era in which women are commemorated and included in the narratives we were excluded from just decades ago, we are still nowhere near the finish line of recognition. This book can help change that, and it inspires me. I believe *Women of Interest* can unite women in embracing how far we've come, while simultaneously helping us laugh at our trials, errors, accomplishments, and feats. After all, humor is truly the most universal language.

I hope you join me in celebrating us. Yes, you and I and every other woman out there living an oh-so-extraordinary, yet ordinary, life. It is so important for us women to realize that we do not have to accomplish stereotypically extraordinary feats on a daily basis to be considered great. Waking up each morning and making coffee is great! Spending a few weeks dedicated to gardening is great! Trying out-of-the-box vegan recipes is great! Reading a trivia book all about women in one or even a few sittings is great! Most importantly, I hope this book brings you joy and lights up your face with a soft smile in commemoration of our collective greatness. Now let's begin the celebration!

Sincerely,

BECCA ANDERSON
Author of *Badass Affirmations* and
The Book of Awesome Women

SELECTED
BIBLIOGRAPHY

BOOKS AND PERIODICALS

Achtemeier, Philip J., general editor. *Harper's Bible Dictionary*. San Francisco: HarperSanFrancisco, 1985.

Anderson, Becca. *The Book of Awesome Women Writers*. Miami: Mango Publishing, 2020.

Ash, Russell. *Fantastic Book of 1001 Lists*. New York: DK Publishing, 1999.

Ballenger, Seale. *Hell's Belles*. San Francisco, CA: Conari Press, 1997.

Barber, Hoyt and Harry L. *The Book of Bond: James Bond*. Nipomo, CA: Cyclone Books, 1999.

The Bathroom Readers' Institute. *Uncle John's Legendary Lost Bathroom Reader*. Ashland, OR: Bathroom Readers' Press, 1999.

————. *Uncle John's Giant 10th Anniversary Bathroom Reader*. Ashland, OR: Bathroom Readers' Press, 1997.

Birnbaum, Cara. "Cosmo's Sexiest Survey Ever." *Cosmopolitan*, March 2001, 197–99.

Bon Appètit. "2001 Reader Survey."

Brinkrant, Ruth. *Fascinating Facts about Love, Sex & Marriage*. New York: Crown, 1982.

Charlton, Mark B. *The Great American Bathroom Reader*. New York: James Charlton Associates, 1997.

————. *The Great American Bathroom Book III*. Salt Lake City, UT: Compact Classics, 1994.

Cohl, Aaron. *The Book of Mosts*. New York: St. Martin's Press, 1997.

DeKay, James. *The Left-Hander's Handbook*. New York: MJF Books, 1966, 1979, 1985, 1996.

The Diagram Group. *Funky, Freaky FACTS Most People Don't Know*. New York: Sterling Publishing Company, 1997.

Dolan, Deidre. "Farewell, Our Lovely." *Premiere*, July 2001, 18–19.

Donati, Annabelle. *I Wonder Which Snake Is the Longest*. Norfolk, CT: Graymont Enterprises, 1999.

Duffy, Bob. "Hidden Treasure." *Boston Globe*, June 24, 2001.

Feldman, David. *A World of Imponderables*. New York: Gallahad Books, 2000.

──────. *Who Put the Butter in Butterfly?* New York: Harper & Row, 1989.

Ferrill, Steven J. *The Cultural Literacy Trivia Guide*. St. Louis, MO: Independent Publishing Corporation, 2001.

George, Margaret. *The Memoirs of Cleopatra*. New York: St. Martin's Press, 1997.

Goldwin, Martin. *How a Fly Walks Upside Down...And Other Curious Facts*. New York: Wing Books, 1979.

Hoffman, David. *Who Knew?* Kansas City, MO: Andrews McNeel, 2000.

Jones, Beth. *Baby Boomer Trivia*. Tulsa, OK: Trade Life Books, 2000.

Jordan, Deane. *1,001 Facts Someone Screwed Up*. Atlanta, GA: Longstreet Press, 1993.

──────. *1,001 MORE Facts Someone Screwed Up*. Atlanta, GA: Longstreet Press, 1997.

Josephs, Katherine. "Price Points." *Money*, July 2001, 24.

Kelly, Sean and Rosemary Rogers. *Saints Preserve Us!* New York: Random House, 1993.

Kipfer, Barbara Ann. *The Order of Things*. New York: Random House, 1996, 1998.

Knight, Brenda. *Wild Women and Books*. San Francisco, CA: Conari Press, 2000.

Korda, Michael. *Another Life*. New York: Random House, 1999.

Lampley, Jonathan Malcolm, Ken Beck, and Jim Clark. *The Amazing, Colossal Book of Horror Trivia*. Nashville, TN: Cumberland House, 1999.

Laudan, Larry. *Danger Ahead*. New York: John Wiley & Sons, 1997.

Lee, Stan. *The Best of the World's Worst*. New York: Gramercy Books, 1994.

Lo Bello, Nino. *The Incredible Book of Vatican Facts and Papal Curiosities: A Treasury of Trivia*. Liguori, MO: Liguori Publications, 1998.

Madden, Annette. *In Her Footsteps*. San Francisco, CA: Conari Press, 2001.

McBride, Joseph. *The Book of Movie Lists*. Chicago: Contemporary Books, 1999.

McLain, Bill. *What Makes Flamingos Pink?* New York: HarperResource, 2001.

McWhirter, Norris. *Book of Millennium Records*. London: Virgin, 1999.

Melymuka, Kathleen. "Stressed-Out IT Women Tempted to Quit, Survey Finds." *Computerworld*, March 15, 2001, *computerworld.com*.

————. "If Girls Don't Get IT, IT Won't Get Girls." *Computerworld*, January 8, 2001, *computerworld.com*.

Mingo, Jack and Erin Barrett. *Just Curious, Jeeves*. Emeryville, CA: Ask Jeeves, 2000.

Morgan, Tom. *Saints*. San Francisco: Chronicle Books, 1994.

Orloff, Erica and JoAnn Baker. *Dirty Little Secrets*. New York: St. Martin's Press, 2001.

Petras, Ross and Kathryn. *Stupid Celebrities*. Kansas City, MO: Andrews McNeel, 1998.

————. *Stupid Sex*. New York: Doubleday, 1998.

Richardson, Matthew. *Whose Bright Idea Was That?* New York: Kodansha International, 1997.

Rilly, Cheryl. *Great Moments in Sex*. New York: Three Rivers Press, 1999.

Rosch, Leah. "What Mothers and Grandmothers Really Think of One Another." *Child*, May 2001, 43.

Rosso, Julee and Sheila Lukins. *The New Basics Cookbook*. New York: Workman Publishing, 1989.

Ryan, M. J. *365 Health & Happiness Boosters*. San Francisco, CA: Conari Press, 2000.

Schwartz, Kit. *The Female Member*. New York: St. Martin's Press, 1988.

Settel, Joanne. *Exploding Ants*. New York: Athenaeum, 1999.

Solle, Dorothee. *Great Women of the Bible in Art and Literature*. Grand Rapids, MI: William B. Eerdmans Publishing Company, 1994.

Stephens, Autumn. *Drama Queens*. San Franscisco, CA: Conari Press, 1998.

————. *Out of the Mouths of Babes*. San Franscisco, CA: Conari Press, 2001.

Strodder, Chris. *Swinging Chicks of the '60s*. San Rafael, CA: Cedco Publishing, 2000.

Sutton, Caroline. *How Do They Do That?* New York: Quill, 1982.

Sutton, Caroline and Kevin Markey. *More How DO They Do That?* New York: Quill, 1993.

Thurman, Judith. "The Queen Himself." *New Yorker*, May 7, 2001, 72–77.

Tibballs, Geoff. *The Best Book of Lists Ever!* Anne's Court, London: Carlton, 1999.

Trombly, Maria. "Wall St. IT Women Trail Men in Pay." *Computerworld*, February 12, 2001, computerworld.com.

Underhill, Paco. *Why We Buy*. New York: Simon and Schuster, 1999.

Ventura, Varla. *Sheroes*. San Franscisco, CA: Conari Press, 1998.

Voorhees, Don. *Thoughts for the Throne: The Ultimate Bathroom Book of Useless Information*. New York: Carol Publishing Group, 1995.

Wang, Holman. *Bathroom Stuff*. Naperville, IL: Sourcebooks, 2001.

Welch, Leslee. *Sex Facts*. New York: Carol Publishing Group, 1992.

Wells, Susan. *The Olympic Spirit: 100 Years of the Games*. Atlanta, GA: Tehabi Books, 1996.

Yalom, Marilyn. *A History of the Wife*. New York: HarperCollins, 2001.

Zotti, Ed. *Know It All!* New York: Ballantine Books, 1993.

WEBSITES

- almanac.com
- bartleby.com
- brittannica.com
- cuisinenet.com
- factmonster.com
- vintagevixen.com

Alicia Alvrez is a San Francisco Bay Area writer, a woman's studies scholar, and an avid trivia fan. She specializes in compiling facts about women and writing for and about women. She is also the author of *The Ladies' Room Reader*, *The Ladies' Room Reader Revisited*, and *Mama Says: The Best Advice from Some of the World's Best Mothers*.

Conari Press

Conari Press, an imprint of Mango Publishing, was established in 1987 and publishes books on topics ranging from psychology, spirituality, and women's history to sexuality, parenting, and personal growth. Our main goal is to publish quality books that will make a difference in people's lives—both how we feel about ourselves and how we relate to one another.

Mango Publishing, established in 2014, publishes an eclectic list of books by diverse authors—both new and established voices—on topics ranging from business, personal growth, women's empowerment, LGBTQ studies, health, and spirituality to history, popular culture, time management, decluttering, lifestyle, mental wellness, aging, and sustainable living. We were recently named 2019's #1 fastest growing independent publisher by *Publishers Weekly.* Our success is driven by our main goal, which is to publish high quality books that will entertain readers as well as make a positive difference in their lives.

Our readers are our most important resource; we value your input, suggestions, and ideas. We'd love to hear from you—after all, we are publishing books for you!

Please stay in touch with us and follow us at:

- Facebook: Mango Publishing
- Twitter: @MangoPublishing
- Instagram: @MangoPublishing
- LinkedIn: Mango Publishing
- Pinterest: Mango Publishing

Sign up for our newsletter at www.mangopublishinggroup.com and receive a free book!

Join us on Mango's journey to reinvent publishing, one book at a time.